"Congress shall make no law . . . abridging the freedom of speech, or of the press."

First Amendment to the U.S. Constitution

The basic foundation of our democracy is the First Amendment guarantee of freedom of expression. The Opposing Viewpoints series is dedicated to the concept of this basic freedom and the idea that it is more important to practice it than to enshrine it.

Feminism

Christina Fisanick, Book Editor

GREENHAVEN PRESS
An imprint of Thomson Gale, a part of The Thomson Corporation

Detroit • New York • San Francisco • New Haven, Conn. • Waterville, Maine • London

THOMSON
─────✦─────™
GALE

Christine Nasso, *Publisher*
Elizabeth Des Chenes, *Managing Editor*

© 2008 The Gale Group.

Star logo is a trademark and Gale and Greenhaven Press are registered trademarks used herein under license.

For more information, contact:
Greenhaven Press
27500 Drake Rd.
Farmington Hills, MI 48331-3535
Or you can visit our Internet site at http://www.gale.com

Articles in Greenhaven Press anthologies are often edited for length to meet page requirements. In addition, original titles of these works are changed to clearly present the main thesis and to explicitly indicate the author's opinion. Every effort is made to ensure that Greenhaven Press accurately reflects the original intent of the authors. Every effort has been made to trace the owners of copyrighted material.

Cover photograph reproduced by permission of © Playboy Archive/Corbis.

LIBRARY OF CONGRESS CATALOGING-IN-PUBLICATION DATA

Feminism / Christina Fisanick, book editor.
    p. cm. -- (Opposing Viewpoints)
    Includes bibliographical references and index.
    ISBN-13: 978-0-7377-3769-1 (hardcover)
    ISBN-13: 978-0-7377-3770-7 (pbk.)
    1. Feminism. 2. Women's rights. I. Fisanick, Christina.
    HQ1155.F44 2008
    305.42--dc22
                                                           2007029714

ISBN-10: 0-7377-3769-7 (hardcover)
ISBN-10: 0-7377-3770-0 (pbk.)

Printed in the United States of America
10 9 8 7 6 5 4 3 2 1

Contents

Chapter 3: How Has Feminism Affected Women's Roles in the Workplace?

Chapter 4: How Has Feminism Affected Women's Roles in the Home?

Why Consider Opposing Viewpoints?

> *"The only way in which a human being can make some approach to knowing the whole of a subject is by hearing what can be said about it by persons of every variety of opinion and studying all modes in which it can be looked at by every character of mind. No wise man ever acquired his wisdom in any mode but this."*
>
> *John Stuart Mill*

In our media-intensive culture it is not difficult to find differing opinions. Thousands of newspapers and magazines and dozens of radio and television talk shows resound with differing points of view. The difficulty lies in deciding which opinion to agree with and which "experts" seem the most credible. The more inundated we become with differing opinions and claims, the more essential it is to hone critical reading and thinking skills to evaluate these ideas. Opposing Viewpoints books address this problem directly by presenting stimulating debates that can be used to enhance and teach these skills. The varied opinions contained in each book examine many different aspects of a single issue. While examining these conveniently edited opposing views, readers can develop critical thinking skills such as the ability to compare and contrast authors' credibility, facts, argumentation styles, use of persuasive techniques, and other stylistic tools. In short, the Opposing Viewpoints series is an ideal way to attain the higher-level thinking and reading skills so essential in a culture of diverse and contradictory opinions.

In addition to providing a tool for critical thinking, Opposing Viewpoints books challenge readers to question their own strongly held opinions and assumptions. Most people form their opinions on the basis of upbringing, peer pressure, and personal, cultural, or professional bias. By reading carefully balanced opposing views, readers must directly confront new ideas as well as the opinions of those with whom they disagree. This is not to simplistically argue that everyone who reads opposing views will—or should—change his or her opinion. Instead, the series enhances readers' understanding of their own views by encouraging confrontation with opposing ideas. Careful examination of others' views can lead to the readers' understanding of the logical inconsistencies in their own opinions, perspective on why they hold an opinion, and the consideration of the possibility that their opinion requires further evaluation.

Evaluating Other Opinions

To ensure that this type of examination occurs, Opposing Viewpoints books present all types of opinions. Prominent spokespeople on different sides of each issue as well as well-known professionals from many disciplines challenge the reader. An additional goal of the series is to provide a forum for other, less-known, or even unpopular viewpoints. The opinion of an ordinary person who has had to make the decision to cut off life support from a terminally ill relative, for example, may be just as valuable and provide just as much insight as a medical ethicist's professional opinion. The editors have two additional purposes in including these less-known views. One, the editors encourage readers to respect others' opinions—even when not enhanced by professional credibility. It is only by reading or listening to and objectively evaluating others' ideas that one can determine whether they are worthy of consideration. Two, the inclusion of such viewpoints encourages the important critical thinking skill of objectively evaluating an author's credentials and bias. This evaluation will illuminate an author's reasons for taking a particular stance on an issue and will aid in readers' evaluation of the author's ideas.

It is our hope that these books will give readers a deeper understanding of the issues debated and an appreciation of the complexity of even seemingly simple issues when good and honest people disagree. This awareness is particularly important in a democratic society such as ours in which people enter into public debate to determine the common good. Those with whom one disagrees should not be regarded as enemies but rather as people whose views deserve careful examination and may shed light on one's own.

Thomas Jefferson once said that "difference of opinion leads to inquiry, and inquiry to truth." Jefferson, a broadly educated man, argued that "if a nation expects to be ignorant and free . . . it expects what never was and never will be." As individuals and as a nation, it is imperative that we consider the opinions of others and examine them with skill and discernment. The Opposing Viewpoints series is intended to help readers achieve this goal.

David L. Bender and Bruno Leone,
Founders

Introduction

> *"Feminism is the radical notion that women are human beings."*
>
> —*Cheris Kramerae,*
> A Feminist Dictionary

According to a 2005 poll conducted by CBS News, it is a tough time to be a feminist. Although the majority of women polled believe that the women's movement had helped improve their opportunities above those of their mothers' generation, 70 percent of them did not consider themselves to be feminists. This data reflects what has become a growing number of women who have distanced themselves from the label "feminist." It is not uncommon for women, especially young women, to begin sentences about the rights of women with the phrase, "I am not a feminist, but . . ." Regrettably, feminism has become the new f-word.

Throughout its history, feminism has fought against incredible backlash, but perhaps none so great as the current state of affairs. Many women in 2007 either do not feel that feminism is necessary or they do not want to be associated with what they believe it represents. Common media stereotypes of feminists depict man-hating, angry women. While certainly some feminists are angry and some hate men, not all feminists do. In fact, according to Kristin Rowe-Finkbeiner in *The F-Word: Feminism in Jeopardy*, feminism "simply means the belief in the social, political, and economic equality of the sexes."

Part of the reason why some women shy away from the feminist label is that feminists are often portrayed negatively by the media. It is not uncommon for college-aged women to report that when they think of feminists, they imagine "lesbian, man-haters." Of course, this stereotype has been per-

14

petuated over the years because it makes people watch the news. At the same time, other public figures have misrepresented feminists for their own gains. In a now-famous statement that appeared in the *Washington Post* in 1992, Christian evangelist Pat Robertson said that feminists "leave their husbands, kill their children, practice witchcraft, destroy capitalism, and become lesbians." Obviously, few people, especially young women, would want to identify with such an image.

In fact, many young women have turned away from feminism or have never been turned on to it because of the risk of social stigmatization. Some young women worry that they will be unappealing to the opposite sex if they show too much support for feminism. They fear that they will become outcasts. In an article in the U.K. zine, *the f-word*, Emma Cosh speaks to this fear when she writes that "the risk for standing up for our beliefs feels all too real." These young women feel that they must risk too much socially both in their peer groups and within their families if they outwardly agree with and call themselves feminists.

At the same time, Rowe-Finkbeiner found in her research that as much as young women want to belong to social groups, they do not like to be labeled. More than 68 percent of the campus women she surveyed for her book reported not liking being labeled by political party or by other ideological names. As Rowe-Finkbeiner notes, "They dislike labels because they believe they are inaccurate, stereotyping, and insensitive; the labels that define sexuality (straight, lesbian, bisexual, etc.) and 'feminist' grated the most." In other words, even if these women believe in the ideals behind the feminist movement, they do not want to take on the label feminist because the whole idea of labels is troubling.

In order to encourage growth and power in the women's movement, some women have suggested retiring the word "feminist" and adopting a new term that has less negative connotations. Some women have suggested words like "humanist" or "womanist." In an interview with salon.com writer Rebecca Traister, famed feminist and author of the 1970s bestseller *Fear of Flying*, Erica Jong argues that it might be time for a new term: "If we need to change the name to get people involved, we should." Other women, however, have sought to reclaim "feminism" from its current, negative image. The recent publication of several books and zines referring to feminism as the f-word as a way of recovering it from stigmatization has led many young women to embrace the term for their own generation. In her article, "War of Words," Kate Townsend discusses this endeavor by saying that "we need feminism in order to talk about feminism. We need to talk about it in order to practice it. And we need to practice it in order to actually affect the world with it."

It remains to be seen if the next generation of young women will embrace or reject the label feminist. Certainly, they will continue as the women before them to desire equality for women. The authors in *Opposing Viewpoints: Feminism* debate how they will achieve that goal in the following chapters: What is Feminism?, How Has Feminism Impacted Female Sexuality and Reproduction?, How Has Feminism Affected Women's Roles in the Workplace?, and How Has Feminism Affected Women's Roles in the Home? It is how the young women of today and tomorrow respond to these debates that will mold the futures of women worldwide.

CHAPTER 1

What is Feminism?

Chapter Preface

In October 2006 the feminist blogosphere was abuzz about a photo in which a young woman appeared with former President Bill Clinton wearing a sweater that some bloggers thought was too revealing. In response to these comments, Amanda, a blogger at Pandagon.com, posted an altered photo with the young woman wearing a burka, an Islamic body covering worn by women. Many bloggers protested that using the burka as a symbol of anti-woman ideals was not only offensive to Islamic women who take their faith seriously, but also because it questions the supposition that women who wear burkas can be feminists. All of this heated discussion eventually led to a much broader question: "What does a feminist look like?"

On the one hand, some feminists believe that women who make decisions about their appearances, including style of dress, to wear makeup or not, to shave their legs or not, and so forth, based on the way in which society, and especially men, see them is oppressive. In fact, shortly after the fall of the Taliban in 2001, an article by American feminists Joan Jacobs Brumberg and Jacqueline Jackson published in the *Boston Globe* took on this issue. According to them, "The burka and the bikini represent opposite ends of the political spectrum but each can exert a noose-like grip on the psyche and physical health of girls and women." Therefore, women such as Brumberg and Jackson might argue that feminists who make choices about their outward appearances that are perceived to be oppressive are not supporting the rights of women at all.

On the other hand, some feminists argue that by dictating that certain clothing and hair styles have only one meaning takes away women's rights to free expression, especially in regards to sexuality. They argue that it is a woman's right to choose what she wears and how she wears it. In an article on

Alternative News Network, Kate Murray-Browne argues that "Feminism should have no 'dress code.'" She asserts that by imposing some kind of strict value system on the meaning of outward appearances, some feminists attempt to control the kind of women who can be part of the movement.

Ultimately, most feminists would agree that it does not matter whether a woman wears makeup and stiletto heels or a plaid shirt and loafers as long as she agrees that women should have equal rights. Many contemporary feminists, including some of the authors in this chapter, have embraced the notion that there are many types of feminism, including multicultural feminism, socialist feminism, conservative feminism, and lesbian feminism to name a few. Naturally, these women would argue that there are also multiple kinds of feminists who look different and act different from one another. To advance this notion, the Feminist Majority Foundation began selling t-shirts in 2003 emblazoned with the slogan, "This is what a feminist looks like."

> *"Feminism' is an umbrella term for a range of views about injustices against women."*

Feminism Is a Complicated Concept

Sally Haslanger and Nancy Tuana

In the following viewpoint Sally Haslanger, professor of philosophy at MIT, and Nancy Tuana, professor of philosophy at Penn State University, offer an overview of the diverse perceptions of contemporary feminism. They argue that it is more illuminating to examine feminism as a system of beliefs than to see it in terms of stages or movements. In addition to pointing out contradictory views of feminism in popular culture, Haslanger and Tuana explore some of the disagreements among feminists about the nature of feminism. Ultimately, they argue, feminism is about bringing an end to injustices against women.

As you read, consider the following questions:

1. What did "feminism" mean in the mid-1800s?
2. What are the differences between the first, second, and third waves of feminism?

Sally Haslanger and Nancy Tuana, "Topics in Feminism," *Stanford Encyclopedia of Philosophy*, Spring 2007 Edition, Edward N. Zalta (ed.), http://plato.stanford.edu/archives/spr2007/entries/feminism-topics. Copyright © 2004 by Sally Haslanger and Nancy Tuana. Reproduced by permission.

3. Why was "womanism" used instead of "feminism" during the 1860s–1880s?

The term "feminism" has many different uses and its meanings are often contested. For example, some writers use the term "feminism" to refer to a historically specific political movement in the US and Europe; other writers use it to refer to the belief that there are injustices against women, though there is no consensus on the exact list of these injustices. Although the term "feminism" has a history in English linked with women's activism from the late 19th century to the present, it is useful to distinguish feminist ideas or beliefs from feminist political movements, for even in periods where there has been no significant political activism, around women's subordination, individuals have been concerned with and theorized about justice for women. . . .

In the mid-1800s the term "feminism" was used to refer to "the qualities of females," and it was not until after the First International Women's Conference in Paris in 1892 that the term, following the French term féministe, was used regularly in English for a belief in and advocacy of equal rights for women based on the idea of the equality of the sexes. Although the term "feminism" in English is rooted in the mobilization for woman suffrage in Europe and the US during the late 19th and early 20th century, of course efforts to obtain justice for women did not begin or end with this period of activism. So some have found it useful to think of the women's movement in the US as occurring in "waves." On the wave model, the struggle to achieve basic political rights during the period from the mid-19th century until the passage of the Nineteenth Amendment in 1920 counts as "First Wave" feminism. Feminism waned between the two world wars, to be "revived" in the late 1960's and early 1970's as "Second Wave" feminism. In this second wave, feminists pushed beyond the early quest for political rights to fight for greater equality across the board, e.g., in education, the workplace, and at home. More recent transformations of feminism have resulted in a "Third Wave". Third Wave feminists often critique Second Wave feminism for its lack of attention to the differences among women due to race, ethnicity, class, nationality, religion, and emphasize "identity" as a site of gender struggle.

However, some feminist scholars object to identifying feminism with these particular moments of political activism, on the grounds that doing so eclipses the fact that there has been resistance to male domination that should be considered "feminist" throughout history and across cultures: i.e., feminism is not confined to a few (White) women in the West over the past century or so. Moreover, even considering only relatively recent efforts to resist male domination in Europe and the US, the emphasis on "First" and "Second" Wave feminism ignores the ongoing resistance to male domination between the 1920's and 1960's and the resistance outside mainstream politics, particularly by women of color and working-class women.

One strategy for solving these problems would be to identify feminism in terms of a set of ideas or beliefs rather than participation in any particular political movement. As we saw above, this also has the advantage of allowing us to locate isolated feminists whose work was not understood or appreciated during their time. But how should we go about identifying a core set of feminist beliefs? Some would suggest that we should focus on the political ideas that the term was apparently coined to capture, viz., the commitment to women's equal rights. This acknowledges that commitment to and advocacy for women's rights has not been confined to the Women's Liberation Movement in the West. But this too raises controversy, for it frames feminism within a broadly liberal approach to political and economic life. Although most feminists would probably agree that there is some sense of "rights" on which achieving equal rights for women is a necessary condition for feminism to succeed, most would also argue that this would not be sufficient. This is because women's oppression under male domination rarely if ever consists solely of depriving women of political and legal "rights," but also extends into the structure of our society and the content of our culture, and permeates our consciousness.

Is there any point, then, to asking what feminism is? Given the controversies over the term and the politics of circumscribing the boundaries of a social movement, it is sometimes tempting to think that the best we can do is to articulate a set of disjuncts that capture a range of feminist beliefs. However, at the same time it can be both intellectually and politically valuable to have a schematic framework that enables us to map at least some of our points of agreement and disagreement. We'll begin here by considering some of the basic elements of feminism as a political position or set of beliefs. . . .

Normative and Descriptive Components

In many of its forms, feminism seems to involve at least two groups of claims, one normative and the other descriptive. The normative claims concern how women ought (or ought not) to be viewed and treated and draw on a background conception of justice or broad moral position; the descriptive claims concern how women are, as a matter of fact, viewed and treated, alleging that they are not being treated in accordance with the standards of justice or morality invoked in the normative claims. Together the normative and descriptive claims provide reasons for working to change the way things are; hence, feminism is not just an intellectual but also a political movement.

So, for example, a liberal approach of the kind already mentioned might define feminism (rather simplistically here) in terms of two claims:

i. (Normative) Men and women are entitled to equal rights and respect.

ii. (Descriptive) Women are currently disadvantaged with respect to rights and respect, compared with men [. . . in such and such respects and due to such and such conditions . . .].

On this account, that women and men ought to have equal rights and respect is the normative claim, and that women are denied equal rights and respect functions here as the descriptive claim. Admittedly, the claim that women are disadvantaged with respect to rights and respect is not a "purely descriptive" claim since it plausibly involves an evaluative component. However, our point here is simply that claims of this sort concern what is the case not what ought to be the case. Moreover, as indicated by the ellipsis above, the descriptive component of a substantive feminist view will not be articulable in a single claim, but will involve an account of the specific social mechanisms that deprive women of, e.g., rights and respect. . . .

Disagreements *within* feminism can occur with respect to either the descriptive or normative claims, e.g., feminists differ on what would count as justice or injustice for women (what counts as "equality," "oppression," "disadvantage," what rights should everyone be accorded?), and what sorts of injustice women in fact suffer (what aspects of women's current situation are harmful or unjust?). Disagreements may also lie in the explanations of the injustice: two feminists may agree that women are unjustly being denied proper rights and respect and yet substantively differ in their accounts of how or why the injustice occurs and what is required to end it.

Disagreements between feminists and non-feminists can occur with respect to both the normative and descriptive claims as well, e.g., some non-feminists agree with feminists on the ways women ought to be viewed and treated, but don't see any problem with the way things currently are. Others disagree about the background moral or political views.

Three Components of Feminism

In the most basic sense, feminism is exactly what the dictionary says it is: the movement for social, political, and economic equality of men and women. Public opinion polls confirm that when people are given this definition, 67 percent say they agree with feminism. We prefer to add to that seemingly uncontroversial statement the following: feminism means that women have the right to enough information to make informed choices about their lives. And because "women" is an all encompassing term that includes middle-class white women, rich black lesbians, and working-class straight Asian women, an organic intertwining with movements for racial and economic equality, as well as gay rights, is inherent to the feminist mandate. Some sort of allegiance between women and men is also an important component of equality. After all, equality is a balance between the male and female with the intention of liberating the individual.

Breaking down that one very basic definition, feminism has three components. It is a *movement*, meaning a group working to accomplish specific goals. Those goals are *social and political change*—implying that one must be engaged with the government and law, as well as social practices and beliefs. And implicit to these goals is access to sufficient information to enable women to make responsible choices.

Jennifer Baumgardner and Amy Richards,
Manifesta: Young Women, Feminism, and the Future.
New York: Farrar, Straus, and Giroux, 2000.

In an effort to suggest a schematic account of feminism, [feminist philospher] Susan James characterizes feminism as follows:

Feminism is grounded on the belief that women are oppressed or disadvantaged by comparison with men, and that their oppression is in some way illegitimate or unjustified. Under the umbrella of this general characterization there are, however, many interpretations of women and their oppression, so that it is a mistake to think of feminism as a single philosophical doctrine, or as implying an agreed political program.

James seems here to be using the notions of "oppression" and "disadvantage" as placeholders for more substantive accounts of injustice (both normative and descriptive) over which feminists disagree.

Some might prefer to define feminism in terms of a normative claim alone: feminists are those who believe that women are entitled to equal rights, or equal respect, or . . . (fill in the blank with one's preferred account of injustice), and one is not required to believe that women are currently being treated unjustly. However, if we were to adopt this terminological convention, it would be harder to identify some of the interesting sources of disagreement both with and within feminism, and the term "feminism" would lose much of its potential to unite those whose concerns and commitments extend beyond their moral beliefs to their social interpretations and political affiliations. Feminists are not simply those who are committed in principle to justice for women; feminists take themselves to have reasons to bring about social change on women's behalf.

I'm Not a Feminist But . . .

Taking "feminism" to entail both normative and empirical commitments also helps make sense of some uses of the term "feminism" in recent popular discourse. In everyday conversation it is not uncommon to find both men and women prefixing a comment they might make about women with the caveat, "I'm not a feminist, but.. . ." Of course this qualification might be (and is) used for various purposes, but one persistent usage seems to follow the qualification with some claim that is hard to distinguish from claims that feminists are wont to make. E.g., I'm not a feminist but I believe that women should earn equal pay for equal work; or I'm not a feminist but I'm delighted that first-rate women basketball players are finally getting some recognition in the WNBA. If we see the identification "feminist" as implicitly committing one to both a normative stance about how things should be and an interpretation of current conditions, it is easy to imagine someone being in the position of wanting to cancel his or her endorsement of either the normative or the descriptive claim. So, e.g., one might be willing to acknowledge that there are cases where women have been disadvantaged without wanting to buy any broad moral theory that takes a stance on such things (especially where it is unclear what that broad theory is). Or one might be willing to acknowledge in a very general way that equality for women is a good thing, without being committed to interpreting particular everyday situations as unjust (especially if [it] is unclear how far these interpretations would have to extend). Feminists, however, at least according to popular discourse, are ready to both adopt a broad account of what justice for women would require and interpret everyday situations as unjust by the standards of that account. Those who explicitly cancel their commitment to feminism may then be happy to endorse some part of the view but are unwilling to endorse what they find to be a problematic package.

As mentioned above, there is considerable debate within feminism concerning the normative question: what would count as (full) justice for women? What is the nature of the wrong that feminism seeks to address? E.g., is the wrong that women have been deprived equal rights? Is it that women have been denied equal respect for their differences? Is it that women's experiences have been ignored and devalued? Is it all of the above and more? What framework should we employ to identify and address the issues? . . .

Note, however, that by phrasing the task as one of identifying the wrongs women suffer (and have suffered), there is an implicit suggestion that women as a group can be usefully compared against men as a group with respect to their standing or position in society, and this seems to suggest that women as a group are treated in the same way, or that they all suffer the same injustices, and men as a group all reap the same advantages. But of course this is not the case, or at least not straightforwardly so. As [African American scholar] bell hooks so vividly pointed out, in 1963 when Betty Friedan [in *The Feminine Mystique*] urged women to reconsider the role of housewife and demanded greater opportunities for women to enter the workforce, Friedan was not speaking for working-class women or most women of color. Neither was she speaking for lesbians. Women as a group experience many different forms of injustice, and the sexism they encounter interacts in complex ways with other systems of oppression. In contemporary terms, this is known as the problem of intersectionality. This critique has led some theorists to resist the label "feminism" and adopt a different name for their view. Earlier, during the 1860's–80's, the term "womanism" had sometimes been used for such intellectual and political commitments; more recently, Alice Walker has proposed that a newly defined "womanism" provides a contemporary alternative to "feminism" that better addresses the needs of Black women and women of color more generally. . . .

Where does this leave us? "Feminism" is an umbrella term for a range of views about injustices against women. There are disagreements among feminists about the nature of justice in general and the nature of sexism, in particular, the specific kinds of injustice or wrong women suffer, and the group who should be the primary focus of feminist efforts. Nonetheless, feminists are committed to bringing about social change to end injustice against women, in particular, injustice against women as women.

| *"What's different now, though, is that feminism appears not so much dead as obsolete."*

Feminism Is Obsolete

Kay S. Hymowitz

In the following viewpoint Kay S. Hymowitz, the William E. Simon fellow at the Manhattan Institute and author of Marriage and Caste in America, *argues that feminism is not dead, but it is obsolete. While some activists have noted that young women today fail to claim the title "feminist" because the media have portrayed feminists in inaccurate and unflattering ways, Hymowitz asserts that the real reason they have turned away from feminism has more to do with the movement's disregard and even disrespect for their real life desires and struggles, mainly that of having husbands and children.*

As you read, consider the following questions:

1. According to "The Granddaughters of Feminism" poll, what percentage of adolescent girls believe that women should be paid equally?

2. According to the Census Bureau, what percentage of women with infants were in the workforce in 2000?

3. According to the author, women want to be mothers in what two ways?

When you ask young women today if they think of themselves as feminists, more often than not they will pause for a moment. Then they will answer something like: "Well, I believe in equal pay for equal work," or "Yes, I do believe women should have choices," or "Of course, I believe women should have equal rights."

If these are the principles that define feminism, then we are all feminists now. And the future belongs to feminism, too: a 2001 *American Demographics* survey of adolescent girls entitled "The Granddaughters of Feminism" found that 97 percent believe women should be paid equally, while 92 percent believe "lifestyle choices" should not be limited by sex. Curiously, the war on terror has, if anything, solidified our commitment to women's rights, though orthodox feminists opposed it as another dangerous example of "the cult of masculinity." The sight of women forced to scurry about in sacks brought home to Americans just how much they treasured their freedoms, including those won for women over the past decades. For a remarkable moment, President Bush and Eleanor Smeal of the Feminist Majority, which had long tried to bring Taliban mistreatment of women to the State Department's attention, seemed members of the same party— which, seen against the backdrop of radical Islam, they actually are.

Feminism Is Finished

But how do we explain that pause that comes when you ask women if they consider themselves part of the movement? The truth is, very few Americans are capital "F" Feminists. Polls show that only about a quarter of women are willing to accept the label. Younger women seem no more comfortable with the title than their grandmothers were. Marie Wilson, president of the *Ms* Foundation for Women, has admitted that the elite young women who 20 years ago would have been the generals of the movement are feminists "by attitude . . . [but] are not interested in hearing about organized movements or activism." They mostly do not join [the National Organization of Women] NOW or read *Ms.* magazine. They don't think of themselves as second-class citizens of the patriarchy, or follow "women's issues" in the news, and their marital status seems as likely to predict how they will vote as their sex.

Activists who try to make sense of these young feminists who are not Feminists conclude that the movement has an image problem. The reason so many people believe in feminist goals yet reject the label, they say, is that the media have given us a cartoon picture of liberationists as humorless, Birkenstock-wearing man-haters, our era's version of the old-fashioned spinster. Feminism is still an "unfinished revolution," they say, and young women share its goals. They just don't like the packaging.

But this explanation falls far short. Feminism is not simply suffering from a P.R. problem. It's just over. As in finished.

Supporters will smile and reply that the movement has been read its last rites often during its lifetime. What's different now, though, is that feminism appears not so much dead as obsolete. Yes, it has bred a generation of empowered young women. But rooted in a utopian politics that longs to transcend both biology and ordinary bourgeois longings, it cannot address the realities of the lives that it has helped to change. Young women know this, even if their mothers do not.

Women Want Husbands and Children

Up until a year ago, Amanda Laforge could have served as a poster girl for *Ms.* After graduating from Boston University, she went to American University law school. When she married, she kept her maiden name and her job with the Maryland secretary of state. When she got pregnant, she continued commuting 45 minutes to her new job at the state attorney general's office. When the baby came, she planned to take three months' maternity leave, and then return to the office for a continued climb up the career ladder.

It didn't turn out that way. Instead of becoming super career mom, she quit her job. Yet she shows no symptoms of Oppressed Housewife Syndrome. Isn't she bored? "No. I love it." Does she miss her job? "I do miss working—or at least having colleagues. I've started to look for part-time work." Does she worry that she is not her husband's equal? "I feel superior to my husband," she sniffs. "Women are much more powerful." But won't her career suffer? "I'm struggling with this personally right now. I know I've already compromised my ability to reach the height of my career. But I see a lot of room to make up." Is it so easy to put aside your career? "No, but I had friends whose mothers were career women who just got caught up in something. Now they've worked for 25 or 30 years for X company, and they didn't get to such enormous heights. Would their lives have been that much different if they had worked part-time? I know a lot of fairly educated people," Amanda concludes, "and no one is looking for more time at the office."

It would be a big mistake to see Amanda as a return to 1950s milk-and-cookies motherhood or as evidence of the backlash that Feminists announce with every article by Katie Roiphe. It would be equally wrong to conclude that most young mothers today are quitting work to be with their babies. Many are, but many others are working part-time, or two days a week at the office, say, and three at home. And, yes, many others are going back to work full-time.

But regardless of how they arrange their lives, women like Amanda illustrate a truth that Feminism never anticipated and is still busily denying: after the revolution, women want husbands and children as much as they want anything in life. It's not that the daughters and granddaughters of feminism don't respect those who forgo marriage and motherhood: in the *American Demographics* poll, 89 percent of adolescent girls said a woman does not need a man to be a success, and the percentage of single women between 35 and 44 has increased significantly since 1960. But the vast majority of young women continue to tell pollsters that they want to marry and have children, and they go on to do so. Census experts predict that upward of 90 percent of today's young women will eventually marry, which means, remarkably enough, that women today tie the knot at a rate similar to that of their grandmothers. Moreover, even with the widely publicized decline in fertility in recent decades, a large majority of women will also become mothers; as of 2000, 81 percent of women aged 40 to 44 had given birth to at least one child.

After giving birth, moreover, not many embrace the one preferred feminist solution to liberated motherhood: dropping the baby off at the day-care center for 50 hours a week. According to another *American Demographics* study, having come from broken or latchkey homes, most Gen X-ers think the best arrangement is for one parent to stay home with the kids, a belief that other polls suggest the majority of Americans share. This usually means Mom, even after three decades of feminism and a concerted effort to get fathers to man the nursery. A 1996 Census Bureau report shows that 42 percent of children under five have a parent at home full-time, another 19.4 percent part-time—and the large majority of these parents are women. The latest Census Bureau numbers show that 55 percent of women with infants were in the workforce in 2000, compared with 59 percent two years earlier—the first such decline since 1979.

It's Just a Job

It's no wonder that feminists have a hard time accepting that trends like these could represent what women actually want. After all, feminists of the 1960s and '70s took to the streets on

Feminism Has Lost Its Way

One of the minor casualties of 9/11 was patience for listening to privileged Americans complain, in distinctly anti-American terms, about their privileged American lives. If feminism doesn't want to completely wear out women's patience—and men's, too—it had better find a new agenda. Perhaps one that is, to start with, less blatantly foolish, and more engaged with the issues that women regularly tell pollsters they care most about: crime, the economy, child care, balancing work and motherhood, their children's schools. It might help if organized feminism recognized that, among other things, legal equality already exists. If feminism wants to become vital again, it must first acknowledge the successes that it helped to achieve.

Catherine Seipp, "You've Lost Your Way, Baby,"
www.reason.com, Summer 2002.

the premise that women wanted to escape from the prison house of the bourgeois home and take up positions in the office and the boardroom, where the real power lies. Women consigned to the role of housewife and mother measured out their days with baby spoons and dirty socks, but work, it seemed to these followers of Betty Friedan, would give them adventure, self-expression, freedom. In the seventies, the offices of *Ms.* and other feminist organizations sported signs proclaiming women working! . . .

Such talk has about as much resonance as "Remember the *Maine!*" for younger women. For one thing, the romance of work—what might be called the feminist mystique—has faded. Young women, as more than one I interviewed put it, are far more likely to feel pressure to be "super career women" than to play Ozzie's Harriet. That doesn't mean that those fortunate enough to have challenging jobs don't take great pride in their accomplishments or enjoy the intellectual stimulation they get at the office. And it doesn't mean that there aren't plenty of young women as fiercely ambitious as Duddy Kravitz [the protagonist in a 1959 Modecai Richler novel]. But many are put off by the single-minded careerism they associate with feminism. . . .

Remember also that the majority of women in their twenties and thirties watched their own mothers go to work but didn't see adventurers and heroines. They saw tired women complaining about their bosses and counting the days until the next vacation, just as women their mothers' age saw their fathers doing. And they know from personal experience that taking a meeting with a client or lunching with colleagues involves every bit as much of the role-playing that feminists wanted to escape. "I worked 60 hours a week from the time I got out of college till I got pregnant," one Boston-area 30-year-old marketing executive said. "I was tired of it. My job is not emotionally fulfilling. I like it, but it's just a job." . . .

Single women, especially those in their later twenties and early thirties, have other reasons to feel impatient with the feminist mystique. They followed the careerist script to a tee: they worked until 10 pm, got flashy jobs, fought for promotions. Meanwhile, they had sex when they felt like it, indifferent to whether their partner was husband material or not; they lived with their boyfriends, shrugged when that didn't work out, and moved on to the next one. But after some years of this, many are surprised to find that the single life is less like *Sex and the City* than *The Apartment*. . . .

Motherhood and Feminism

These younger women are especially peeved that, in promoting female independence, feminism denied biological realities that now loom large. Feminists often like to talk about the "click"—the moment when a woman experiences discrimination so clearly that she sees her whole life in a radically new light. For a lot of younger women, the "click" moment has now arrived in a totally unexpected form. With the torrent of media coverage following the recent publication of Sylvia Ann Hewlett's *Creating a Life*—publicity that focused on the fertility problems of older high-achieving women—everything looks different. For just as there are no atheists in foxholes, there are no feminists in the throes of fertility anxiety. . . .

And here we come to the primary reason for feminism's descent into irrelevance. Whereas most young women will at some point want babies like they want food, for feminists, motherhood is the ten-ton boulder in the path of genuine liberation. It mucks up ambition, turning fabulous heroines of the workplace—killer lawyers, 24/7 businesswomen, and ruthless senator wannabes—into bourgeois wifies and mommies. It hinders absolute equality, since women with children don't usually crash through glass ceilings. They resist traveling three days a week to meet with hotshot clients; they look at their watches frequently and make a lot of personal phone calls. . . .

Feminists deal with the unsettling fact that, even after the revolution, women persist in wanting to be mothers in two ways. The first tack is simple denial. Amazingly, given young women's preoccupation with how to balance work and motherhood, neither NOW nor the Feminist Majority, the movement's two most influential organizations, includes maternity leave, flex time, or even day care on its list of vital issues.

The other tack, favored by academic feminists, is a more complex denial. Yes, women may want babies, they concede, but that doesn't mean they want motherhood—at least not motherhood as it has been "constructed" by the patriarchy throughout history. For these theorists, only a social arrangement that makes men and women exactly equal co-parents—at work precisely the same number of hours, and taking care of the children precisely the same number of hours—is acceptable. In a recent article in *The American Prospect*, Janet Gornick averaged out the number of hours worked by mothers of children under three (23) and those worked by fathers (44) and proclaimed the egalitarian goal: both Mom and Dad should work 33.5 hours a week. It is not enough to give men and women more flexibility and choices about how to organize their lives; the goal is "unbending gender," as American University law professor Joan Williams puts it in her book of that title. Williams rejects what she calls "choice rhetoric"; a woman who thinks she is freely choosing to stay home is just fooling herself, in thrall to the "ideology of domesticity." . . .

Little wonder that few women in their twenties and thirties seek to complete this so-called unfinished revolution. They don't yearn for the radical transformation of biological restraints and bourgeois aspirations devoutly wished by stalwarts. Even those few who want more androgynous sex roles for themselves don't wish to impose them on others. Yes, they took women's studies courses—often only to satisfy their college's diversity requirement—but they came away unimpressed. To many of them, feminism today represents not liberation but its opposite: a life that must be lived according to a strict, severe ideology. The younger generation, on the other hand, wants a liberation "that isn't just freedom to choose [but] . . . freedom from having to justify one's choices," as Jennifer Foote Sweeney has put it in *Salon*. In short, they're ready to de-politicize the personal. . . .

> "It [NOW] was a simple act, but it marked the beginning of a lifelong commitment to working for women's equality."

Feminism Is Not Obsolete

Marilyn Gardner

In the following viewpoint, Marilyn Gardner argues that while great advances have been made in the fight for women's equality, there remains a great need for feminism. On the 40⁰ anniversary of the influential group called the National Organization for Women (NOW), feminism activists reflect on the progress women have made over the years on issues like women's education and employment, and men's involvement in child-rearing. Today, women are still faced with challenges such as violence against women, abortion rights, and legalizing same-sex marriage, proof that feminism is still necessary. Marilyn Gardner is a staff writer for The Christian Science Monitor.

As you read, consider the following questions:

1. Leaders note that what issues are drawing new members to NOW?

2. At the time of NOW's creation, what were some of the challenges women faced regarding employment?

3. What is NOW doing to attract the next generation?

As a young editor in the mid-1960s, Karen DeCrow paid $5 in dues to join a fledgling group called the National Organization for Women (NOW). It was a simple act ("I didn't even get a membership card," she recalls), but it marked the beginning of a lifelong commitment to working for women's equality.

NOW 40 Years Later

This weekend [in July 2006] that commitment will take her to Albany, N.Y., where she and more than 800 other members will observe a milestone: NOW's 40th anniversary. Amid balloons and confetti, partygoers will watch a video tracing the group's history. They will also honor founders and past presidents, among them Ms. DeCrow.

"It will be a gala celebration of how we changed the country and the world for women, for children, and definitely for men," says an exuberant DeCrow.

Although NOW puts its membership at 500,000 and counts 550 chapters, the anniversary comes at a time when the group is far less visible than it was in the heady 1970s and 1980s. That is leading both self-described "old-timers" of DeCrow's generation and younger activists to find new ways to work for equality. Leaders note that a growing conservatism in the courts and challenges to reproductive rights are drawing new members.

"I see renewed energy around the country," says Kim Gandy, NOW's president. "There's an increased sense that women need to get involved personally and put themselves on the line to make change, that they can't sit back and say, 'Let Jane do it.'"

Three Letters on a Napkin

Early seeds of change were planted 40 years ago this month [July 2006] when a small band of women gathered at the Washington Hilton seeking ways to enforce a federal law outlawing sex discrimination at work. Betty Friedman, author of "The Feminine Mystique," scribbled three letters—NOW—on a napkin, and an organization was born.

At the time, airline stewardesses, as they were then called, typically lost their jobs when they married, got pregnant, or reached the advanced age of 32. Some waitresses were forbidden to work at night. Women in Utah could not be hired if a job required them to lift more than 15 pounds. Employment ads were segregated by gender.

"Sometimes when I teach or talk to students about the women's movement, I tell them that when I started work, newspaper ads identified jobs as 'Help wanted—male' and 'Help wanted—female,'" says Judy Goldsmith, a former NOW president. "They say, 'Oh, come on,' They don't want to believe it. It's so Neanderthal."

DeCrow remembers other unenlightened attitudes in those early days. "Everyone laughed at us and made fun of us and ignored us. When it seemed we were making progress, they attacked us. It wasn't like the doors were open: 'Oh girls, come in. We're so glad you're calling attention to the fact that there are no women astronauts in the NASA program.' We had barriers everywhere. But it was exciting. People would come from all over the world to meet with us. We could pick our targets, because everything was a target."

Feminism Today

Today discrimination is more subtle and the targets are less obvious, she says. "The issues have matured. We don't have to fight to get women into law school anymore, but overwhelmingly the partners in major firms are still men. Getting into medical school is not an issue. However, at the top there are still problems."

Other issues on NOW's broad-based agenda include violence against women, abortion rights, and legalizing same-sex marriage.

And then there is the family. "One of the wonderful things that has happened is a much greater acceptance and encouragement of men's involvement in child-rearing," Ms. Goldsmith says. "It's taken some of the pressure off men to be the great provider and the rock that everyone leans on."

Yet DeCrow still includes the family on her agenda, saying, "We need a sense that children are a shared responsibility for mothers and fathers. We haven't gotten there yet, although the young fathers of today certainly do a lot more than their dads and grandfathers did."

When Ms. Gandy joined NOW 33 years ago, the most active members were homemakers and students. She describes them as "women of extraordinary intelligence and commitment who hadn't had the opportunity to use those skills in law or medicine or engineering or other professions. They threw their energy into building the movement." Many devoted 30 or 40 hours a week to the work.

That kind of commitment is now rare, Gandy says. Today's membership is mostly made up of women whose work and family obligations leave them little spare time. Activists also have a choice of organizations they can join.

"It used to be just us and NOW," says Clare Giesen, executive director of the National Women's Political Caucus in Washington, formed five years after NOW. "Now there are any number of groups that are addressing niche issues for women—legal issues, family issues." She cites the National Women's Law Center and the National Research Center for Women and Families.

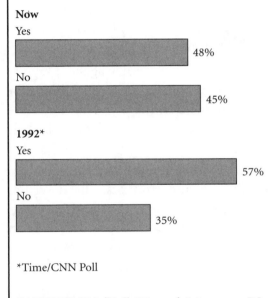

Is There Still a Need for a Strong Women's Movement?

According to a CBS News Poll conducted in May 2005, an overwhelming majority of women say their opportunities to succeed in life are better than the opportunities their mothers had—and most credit the women's movement for making their lives better. But while nearly all women say the status of women has gotten better in this country, they are divided as to whether there is still a need for a strong women's movement.

Now

Yes

48%

No

45%

1992*

Yes

57%

No

35%

*Time/CNN Poll

TAKEN FROM: "Poll: Women's Movement Worthwhile," www .cbsnews.com, October 23, 2005.

The Future of NOW

As NOW's leaders look ahead, they are searching for ways to attract the next generation. Its Young Feminist Task Force, co-chaired by Erin Matson of Minneapolis, includes a dozen members between ages 15 and 29. They advise the national board on issues of concern to young women. This weekend's national conference includes workshops on teen dating violence, music and feminism, and fashion and feminism.

"We are a different generation," Ms. Matson says, "We're much less focused on bylaws and structure and the nuts and bolts of how organizations work. We're figuring out how we work together in a new way, side by side with the people we owe so much of our lives to."

Both generations are keenly aware of the work yet to be done. Women hold only 15 percent of seats in Congress and 14 percent of seats on Fortune 500 boards. On average, they still earn less than men.

"This is not a time for complacency," Goldsmith says.

Some younger women regard this as a transitional time for organizations like NOW.

"I do think NOW still serves a purpose in Washington-based organizing and lobbying," says Jessica Valenti, editor of the website feministing.com. "But younger feminists are exploring new ways of organizing and doing their activism. Hopefully NOW will come along with us."

In the past, she says, activists looked to "large feminist icons" such as Gloria Steinem and Betty Friedan. "Now young women are becoming their own leaders. We don't necessarily need one or two or three feminist icons to show us the way. We're already doing this work." That includes forming grass-roots organizations, magazines, and blogs.

Referring to unfinished work, she says, "It's easy to talk about abortion rights and pay equity, which are obviously important. But poverty is also huge, and child-care is huge, and having to deal with this ridiculous backlash that says, 'Women don't want to work—they want to have lots of babies.'"

In addition, Ms. Valenti says, women must continue to be active in the wider political arena, bringing activism "to electoral politics and to their daily lives."

Feminism Is Still Necessary

Jean Kilbourne, a visiting research scholar at the Wellesley Centers for Women, also sees a need for groups like NOW. "I wish I could say it were no longer necessary, but there are still a lot of issues left to be discussed and resolved," she says. "It's important to remember that these gains are relatively new and not set in stone. We have to be vigilant."

Lillian Ciarrochi, a past president of NOW's Philadelphia chapter, imagines a scenario that would be anything but complacent if those gains are ever threatened. "I think there'll be a revolution. They'll do anything to not lose those rights."

Men Also Fight For Women's Rights

From the beginning, men have served on NOW's board of directors in addition to being members. Robert Seidenberg of Fayetteville, N.Y., is widely considered to be the first male member of the national organization. As a psychiatrist, he became aware of "social and interpersonal" challenges that kept women down. "That propelled me to see what I could do in making things a little better." Describing himself as "very hopeful and very encouraged," he adds, "I see things I never thought were possible."

Dr. Seidenberg offers a radical proposal to honor the woman who wrote those three letters, NOW, on a napkin 40 years ago.

"We don't have any national holiday for a woman in this country yet," he says. "Betty Friedan should be the one. She was not perfect. She was controversial. But the basic thing she did should not be forgotten. She changed America for the better with the liberation of women."

A Reflection on Progress

As Gandy prepares for Saturday's celebration, she reflects on progress.

"Perhaps the greatest changes we've accomplished in the last 40 years are that we've changed hearts and minds, we've changed laws and won lawsuits," she says. "Feminism today is what I hoped it would be 30 years ago. It's my daughters, who are 10 and 13, not just believing they can do anything, but absolutely knowing they can. Unfortunately we haven't come quite that far, but it's so important that our daughters expect equality, because they will demand it when it's not there."

> *"Most Western academic and mainstream feminists have not focused on what I call gender apartheid in the Islamic world."*

Western Feminists Should Fight for Islamic Women

Phyllis Chesler

Phyllis Chesler is an emerita professor of Psychology and Women's Studies at City University of New York, a psychotherapist, and a human rights activist. In the following viewpoint she argues that while Western feminism has accomplished many important goals, it has failed Islamic women by not actively engaging in their liberation. Also, she asserts that feminists must become more involved in world politics as a whole if they are to play a predominant role in the shaping of human rights practices, especially the rights of women.

As you read, consider the following questions:

1. How has feminism been inclusive?
2. According to the author, why are today's feminists seen as marginal?

3. What happened to the author in 1961?

Is feminism really dead? Well, yes and no.

It gives me no pleasure, but someone must finally tell the truth about how feminists have failed their own ideals and their mandate to think both clearly and morally. Only an insider can really do this, someone who cares deeply about feminist values and goals. I have been on the front lines for nearly 40 years, and I feel called upon to explain how many feminists—who should be the first among freedom- and democracy-loving people—have instead become cowardly herd animals and grim totalitarian thinkers. This must be said, and my goal in saying it is a hopeful one. We live at a time when women can and must make a difference in the world.

From the start, feminism has been unfairly, even viciously, attacked. I do not want to do that without cause here. The truth is that in less than 40 years, a visionary feminism has managed to challenge, if not transform, world consciousness.

For example, you can find feminists on every continent who have mounted brave and determined battles against rape, incest, domestic violence, economic and professional inequality, and local "cultural" practices such as Arab honor killings, dowry burnings, female genital mutilation, as well as against the global trafficking in women and children. I don't want to minimize or simplify what feminism has accomplished.

In some ways, feminism has also been inclusive. Feminists are Republicans and Democrats, right-wing conservatives and left-wing radicals; feminists are both religious and anti-religious, anti-abortion and pro-abortion, anti-pornography and pro-pornography, anti-gay-marriage and pro-gay-marriage. Feminists come in all ages and colors; belong to every caste, gender, class, and religion; and live everywhere.

Nevertheless feminists are often perceived as marginal and irrelevant; and in some important ways the perception is accurate.

Lack of Focus on Gender Apartheid

Today the cause of justice for women around the world is as urgent as it has ever been. The plight of both women and men in the Islamic world (and increasingly in Europe) requires a sober analysis of reality and a heroic response. World events have made feminism more important—yet at the same time, feminism has lost much of its power.

To my horror, most Western academic and mainstream feminists have not focused on what I call gender apartheid in the Islamic world, or on its steady penetration of Europe. Such feminists have also failed to adequately wrestle with the complex realities of freedom, tyranny, patriotism, and self-defense, and with the concept of a Just War.

Islamic terrorists have declared jihad against the "infidel West" and against all of us who yearn for freedom. Women in the Islamic world are treated as subhumans. Although some feminists have sounded the alarm about this, a much larger number have remained silent. Why is it that many have misguidedly romanticized terrorists as freedom fighters and condemned both America and Israel as the real terrorists or as the root cause of terrorism? In the name of multicultural correctness (all cultures are equal, formerly colonized cultures are more equal), the feminist academy and media appear to have all but abandoned vulnerable people—Muslims, as well as Christians, Jews, and Hindus—to the forces of reactionary Islamism.

Because feminist academics and journalists are now so heavily influenced by left ways of thinking, many now believe that speaking out against head scarves, face veils, the chador, arranged marriages, polygamy, forced pregnancies, or female genital mutilation is either "imperialist" or "crusade-ist." Postmodernist ways of thinking have also led feminists to believe that confronting narratives on the academic page is as important and world-shattering as confronting jihadists in the flesh and rescuing living beings from captivity.

It is as a feminist—not as an anti-feminist—that I have felt the need to write a book [*The Death of Feminism*] to show that something has gone terribly wrong among our thinking classes. The multicultural feminist canon has not led to independent, tolerant, diverse, or objective ways of thinking. On the contrary. It has led to conformity, totalitarian thinking, and political passivity. Although feminists indulge in considerable nostalgia for the activist 60s and 70s, in some ways they are no different from the rest of the left-leaning academy, which also suffers from the disease of politically correct passivity.

Is women's studies to blame for all this? Well, yes and no. Had the academy been slightly more hospitable to original, radical, and activist feminist energies and had money been plentiful, there might have been no need to ghettoize the study of gender. But that was not the case. In addition, with some exceptions, the kind of feminist faculty members who could survive in academe were, like their male counterparts, far too dutiful.

Navel Gazing

Today feminists are seen as marginal also because of their obsessive focus on "personal" body rights and sexual issues. This is no crime, but it is simply not good enough. It may shock some to hear me say this, but we have other important things on our agenda.

Women can no longer afford to navel gaze—not if they want to play vital roles on the world-historical stage, not if they want to continue to struggle for woman's and humanity's global freedom. And women in America can no longer allow themselves to be rendered inactive, anti-activist, by outdated left and European views of colonial-era racism that are meant to trump and silence concerns about gender.

Of course, not all feminists are passive. Many have been helping the female victims of violence in a hands-on way.

The Form of an Islamic Feminism

Above all, the movement must recognize that, whereas in the West, the mainstream of the women's movement has viewed religion as one of the chief enemies of its progress and well-being, Muslim women view the teachings of Islam as their best friend and supporter. . . .

As far as Muslim women are concerned, the source of any difficulties experienced today is not Islam and its traditions, but certain alien ideological intrusions on our societies, ignorance, and distortion of the true Islam, or exploitation by individuals within the society. . . .

Second, any feminism which is to succeed in an Islamic environment must be one which does not work chauvenistically for women's interest alone. Islamic traditions would dictate that women's progress be achieved in tandem with the wider struggle to benefit all members of the society. The good of the group or totality is always more crucial than the good of any one sector of the society. . . .

Third, Islam is an ideology which influences much more than the ritual life of a people. It is equally affective of their social, political, economic, psychological, and aesthetic life. "Din," which is usually regarded as an equivalent for the English term "religion," is a concept which includes, in addition to those ideas and practices customarily associated in our minds with religion, a wide spectrum of practices and ideas which affect almost every aspect of the daily life of the Muslim individual. . . .

To fail to note this fact, or to fail to be fully appreciative of its importance for the average Muslim—whether male or female—would be to commit any movement advocating improvement of women's position in Islamic hands to certain failure. . . .

Lois Lamya' al Faruqi, "Islamic Traditions and
the Feminist Movement: Confrontation or Cooperation?"
http://www.jannah.org/sisters/feminism.html.

However, this work is not often taught in women's-studies programs, nor does such hands-on work take place on the campus. Many law schools have domestic-violence clinics; most graduate liberal-arts programs do not. Anti-feminist professors in medical and graduate school do not often teach the pioneering work of feminist mental-health professionals.

Some might say that I am being unnecessarily harsh on women who have, indeed, been sounding the alarm about the global rise in fundamentalist misogyny. Perhaps I am. But I think we can really make a difference. I want more of us to put our shoulder to freedom's wheel.

For example, I know that many feminists enjoyed talking about the plight of Afghan women under the Taliban; and why not? This tragedy proved that Feminism 101 was right all along, that men really did oppress women. But few of the televised feminist talking heads wanted to systematically sponsor Afghan women as immigrants or as political refugees. I know because I suggested, privately, that the anti-Taliban American feminists do so. Needless to say, these feminists did not want to launch a military invasion of Afghanistan on behalf of women either. I know. I raised this idea many times. All I got were pitying looks.

Personal Disclosures

Some personal disclosures are now in order.

First, I am a feminist and an American patriot. Yes, one can be both. I am also an internationalist. There is no contradiction here. Finally, I am a religious Jew and am sympathetic to both religious and secular worldviews. Being religious does not compromise my feminism. On the contrary, it gives me the strength and a necessarily humbled perspective to continue the struggle for justice.

Second, Afghanistan matters to me; it has touched my life. Once long ago, in 1961, I was held captive there and kept in purdah for five months; some women were exceptionally kind to me. I will never forget them. I was the young bride of a Western-educated Afghan. My American passport was taken away, and I was thrown into (fairly posh) purdah in Kabul. The unexpected curtailment of my freedom was as awful as it was unexpected. I nearly died there—but I finally escaped.

I believe that my Western feminism was forged in that most beautiful and tragic of countries. And yes, I also understand that America has not yet done all that is necessary to build up the country, that ethnic warlords and drug lords continue to tyrannize civilians, that women are still imprisoned in chadaris and in brutal arranged marriages, with limited access to medical care, education, and employment.

Silence from Feminists

Most academics and activists do not actually do anything; they read, they write, they deliver papers. They may not be able to free slaves or prisoners the way an entering army might, but they can think clearly, and in complex and courageous ways, and they can enunciate a vision of freedom and dignity for women and men. It is crucial, even heroic, that they do so.

Both women and religious minorities in non-Western and Muslim countries, and in an increasingly Islamized Europe, are endangered as never before. In 2004 the Dutch film maker Theo van Gogh was butchered by a jihadist on the streets of Amsterdam for having made a film, *Submission*, which denounced the abuse of women under Koranic Islam. However, the eerie silence both from feminists and film makers about van Gogh's assassination is deafening and disheartening. The same Hollywood loudmouths so quick to condemn and shame President Bush for having invaded Afghanistan and Iraq have, as of this writing, remained silent about the chilling effect that such an assassination in broad daylight can have on academic and artistic freedom.

Perhaps some of the very academics and mainstream feminists whom I am criticizing—but also trying to influence—

will devalue what I am saying. Perhaps they will say that I am no longer a feminist—that I have betrayed feminism, not they. It will not change the truth of what I am saying. My hope is that this will resonate with people of all ages; men and women who are quietly doing feminist work within their profession, and there are many; feminists of faith, and there are also many; both Republicans and Democrats; educators, both here and abroad; and especially with the so-called ordinary people whose lives and freedom are at stake.

"Many American women would be surprised to learn that the history of Arab
feminism is long, layered, and impressive."

Arab Feminism Has
a Long History Without
Western Intervention

Susan Muaddi Darraj

In the following viewpoint, author Susan Muaddi Darraj argues
that Americans have a misrepresented image of Middle Eastern
women, causing a misunderstanding regarding Middle Eastern
feminism. Darraj claims that there is an "astounding disconnection" between how the lives of Arab women are perceived by
Americans and how Arab women actually live. She worries that
by allowing Americans to intervene, Arab women will not have
say in issues concerning their own lives. Susan Muaddi Darraj
has written essays that have appeared in many publications, including New York Stories, Mizna, Pages Magazine, and The
John Hopkins Magazine.

Susan Muaddi Darraj, "Understanding the Other Sister: The Case of Arab Feminism."
Monthly Review, vol. 53, March 2002. Copyright © 2002 by MR Press. Reproduced by
permission of Monthly Review Foundation.

As you read, consider the following questions:

1. How does Darraj describe the misrepresented image of Arab women, as perceived by American women?
2. In Darraj's view, what is the "big sister" manner in which American women have taken to help Arab women, and what is Darraj's concern with this approach?
3. Why do many Middle Eastern women see the veil as irrelevant to the central issue of women's rights, according to Darraj?

One evening, shortly after September 11, I was conducting a college English class when one of my students asked a question about the accumulating body of information on women and Islam. It was one of many questions about the Middle East asked of me in the days after the tragedies; this one was about the veil, and why women in the Middle East "had to wear it." I explained that not all women in the Middle East were Muslim (I myself am a Palestinian Christian), but that even many Muslim women did not veil. However, many did, and for myriad reasons: mostly for personal and religious reasons and, for some, upon compulsion.

The student shook her head sadly, her long ponytail swinging in the air, and offered a comment that made it clear she hadn't really digested what I'd said: "I feel so bad for them all. At least Christian women don't have to walk three steps behind their husbands." She added, "That's so insulting."

False Representation of Arab Women

I understood—and not for the first time—the astounding disconnection between the lives of Arab women, and the lives of Arab women as represented by the American media and entertainment industries, thus as perceived by Americans themselves. Twenty-three years after the publication of Edward Said's seminal book, *Orientalism*, which clarified the historical pattern of misrepresentation and demonization of the Middle East, many Americans continue to purchase wholesale the neatly packaged image of the veiled, meek Arab woman. This pitiful creature follows her husband like a dark shadow, is forced to remain silent and obey her husband at all times, is granted a body only to deliver more children, perhaps even in competition with her husband's other wives.

At some point (like now), the stereotype spins out of control, becoming more wild and ludicrous, like Yeats' ever-widening gyre. The portrayal that persists today, however, is not much of an improvement—if at all—over the portrayal of Arab women in the late 1700s to the early part of the twentieth century. . . .

[Lord] Byron [wrote a] 1812 poem [called] "The Giaour." The Giaour is a warrior who avenges the murder of his beloved, Leila, a girl who dwells in the harem of "Black Hassan" and who is put to death by drowning when it is revealed that she has been unfaithful to the sultan with the Giaour. Pierre Loti's 1879 Aziyade and other poems and works of the time featured a similar theme, that of the Western hero breaking the impasse of the harem, to be rewarded with the passion of women who have been sexually isolated and imprisoned.

What this compilation of wildly exaggerated and self-indulgently fantastical images has resulted in is the creation of a stark contrast between modern American women and modern Arab women. The rise of U.S. feminism in the 1970s and 1980s coincided with the rise of Islam as the "new enemy" of the Western world. Images of the Ayatollah Khomeini in Iran, the Mujahedin in Afghanistan, Qaddafi in Libya, and Yasser Arafat and the PLO [Palestine Liberation Organization] concretized Islam's new role as the author of fear and the enemy of Western democracy, human rights, and especially civil law. And those images of Islam were strategically—almost artistically—painted with glimpses of what Islam did to its own women: it turned them into mute shadows, thus flying in the face of the gender equality and democracy that American feminism claimed as its foundation.

The "Big Sister" Approach

The statements made by my ponytailed student smacked of an underlying assumption that I have heard many times before: we American women have finally succeeded in moving the feminist movement to the top of our nation's list of priorities; now it's time to help our less fortunate sisters. Of course, over the years, American feminism has opened its gates (after much pounding) to other versions of feminism, such as black feminism and other non-white, non-upper-middle-class feminisms. Therefore, the focus on Arab women's issues illustrates the good intentions of American feminism; however, my concern is with the "big sister" manner in which those intentions are manifested. Often, Arab women's voices are excluded from discussions concerning their own lives, and they are to be "informed" about feminism, as if it is an ideology exclusive to American women alone.

In fact, many American women would be surprised to learn that the history of Arab feminism (a term often considered oxymoronic) is long, layered, and impressive. That this is not well understood in the West is not surprising. As Dawn Chatty and Annika Rabo write in the introduction to their edited collection, Organizing Women: Formal and Informal Women's Groups in the Middle East, "Middle Eastern women's groups are not . . . nearly as well documented as in the rest of the world. . . . There is . . . a great deal of antagonism between the Middle East and the West where the latter sees men from the Middle East as suppressing and secluding their women, and where the Middle Easterner underlines the immorality of women in the West." This conflict is one reason why women in the Middle East do not get international attention when organized in groups.

Women's Organizations in the Middle East

Not only do the struggles of Arab feminists have a long history, but over the 1980s and 1990s, as Val Moghadam observes in the same book, "women's NGOs [in the Middle East and North Africa] have grown exponentially and are taking on increasingly important responsibilities in the context of state withdrawal from the provision of social services and in the context of a global trend in the expansion of civil society." Organizations explicitly devoted to women are growing rapidly in Egypt, Tunisia, and Morocco, while more informal service-oriented organizations led by women play some of the same roles in many other Middle Eastern nations. Some of the leading organizations in Egypt include: the New Woman's Group; Arab Women's Publishing House; the Alliance of Arab Women; the Association for the Development and Enhancement of Women; Together; Progressive Women's Union; the group of women who published The Legal Rights of the Egyptian Woman in Theory and Practice, and The Society for the Daughter of the Earth. Taken as a whole, it is a movement that, if allied with U.S. and other feminisms, could improve the lives of women around the world.

The Veil

In 1923, Huda Sha'rawi caused a scandal in Egypt when, upon stepping off a boat that had just returned from Europe (where she had been attending an international feminist conference), she seized the media moment and publicly removed her veil, symbolically denouncing its meaning by throwing it into the sea. However, its meaning has never been universally agreed upon in Arab societies, probably because each society and each historical moment has ascribed a different one to it. During a visit a few years ago to the Gaza Strip, I saw five-year-old girls sheathed in black; I also saw teenaged girls in the West Bank wearing hijabs that flowed to the waistline of their jeans; in fact, the hijab seemed to protect their heads from the hot sun as they played basketball on a full court. What does it all mean? Probably that the veil is not a simple, one-dimensional marker of gender oppression. In *Women and the Middle East and North Africa*, Judith E. Tucker has written of some of the complexity associated with women's choice of dress, which cannot always be attributed directly to patriarchal admonitions:

"Veiling" has become, certainly in the Western view, a touchstone for women's issues. In the 1980s and 1990s, many women in different parts of the Middle East, particularly in urban areas, have donned a new form of "Islamic" dress that includes a long dress or coat and a head scarf often worn without a turban. Although social pressure cannot always be ruled out, many young women appear to choose this form of dress over the alternatives of Western-style dress or various indigenous styles worn by older women. Several explanations have been offered for this trend. First, sociological reasons include the advantages such dress provides for women who study or work in mixed-sex environments. By wearing Islamic dress, women can proclaim their seriousness and avoid the tensions produced by the rapid erosion of sexual segregation while maintaining access to public space. Second, women, like men, have found that the post-independence promises of progress through Western versions of liberalism or socialism have not borne fruit; they signal a "return" to indigenous culture and authenticity as a guide to a better future. Third, there is a rising tide of religiosity in the region that translates, for women and men, into changing dress styles.

Veiling Is a Subject of Intense Debate

Leila Ahmed, author of *Women and Gender in Islam*, asserts that one of the only elements of Qasim Amin's *The Liberation of Women* (1899) that was considered scandalous was his call for the abolition of the veil. Assim declared that the veil was un-Islamic. (It may surprise some Western feminists to know that they are not the first to criticize the veiling of Middle Eastern women, but rather that it has been a subject of intense debate for over a century.) Ahmed said that dialogue about the veil emerged in a heated political and economic context, one in which some Egyptians sought to advance the nation by adopting the Western ways of the British (who still colonized Egypt at this time) and some who believed the same could be realized only by ousting the British and reviving and preserving Islamic traditions. However, Ahmed illustrated clearly that the British "Victorian male establishment" used the idea that Muslim men oppressed Muslim women as a justifiable pretext for its colonization and "civilization" of Muslim countries. As one might expect, the veil, interpreted as a symbol of the silencing of women both by Europeans and by some Egyptians, served well as tangible proof of that oppression.

Many women in the Middle East today see the issue of the veil as an important locus of discussion; I personally know of marriages that have broken up because husbands want their new brides to be "more conservative" and wear the veil. Many other women see the veil as irrelevant to the central issue of women's rights; arguing over it serves to distract from the real problems of women's access to education and health care, and the increasing poverty in which Arab families find themselves.

After September 11

In the days after September 11, I telephoned friends of mine, women I had known for years to inquire if they were experiencing the backlash against Arab- and Muslim-Americans, and anyone else unfortunate enough to resemble them in the minds of people who don't know better. Several of them—all of whom wore the veil—told me that they had been verbally targeted. "I hated stopping at red lights today," said one of my friends, "because the people in the cars next to me would curse at me and give me the finger." After I hung up with her,

I turned on the news and learned about the Pakistani woman who was almost run over in the parking lot of a grocery store; her attacker then followed her into the store and threatened her life. I did not see a picture of the woman, but wondered whether or not she wore any sort of head scarf that would "mark" her as a target.

Middle East and Islam Are Misunderstood

And then I thought of how Islam was terribly misunderstood. The few ritual concessions to tolerance uttered by national figureheads such as President Bush and New York Mayor Rudy Guiliani (scarcely consistent with their own actions) did not erase the fact that most Americans remain unaware of the basic facts about the Middle East and Islam, and women were suffering from that ignorance. For example, while Afghan women and their plight had been singled out by the American media as an example of how backwards the Taliban was (even though, to its credit, American feminism had been criticizing and attempting to educate people about the Taliban since 1996), these same women were also forced to herd their families into refugee camps and/or watch their houses be destroyed in the storm of bombing of Afghanistan that followed the September 11 attacks. The media's popular portrayal of Muslim women as universally helpless and dominated by the patriarchy that continues to exist in Arab culture (as if any society is free of it) has reinforced American perceptions that Arabs and Muslims are degenerate and twisted, thus worthy of domination and bombing.

And yet, if Americans, especially American women, understood the long and enduring history of Arab feminism, then perhaps my students would be able to formulate comments on Arab and Muslim women that were more informed and sensitive. Such commentaries would recognize the complexity of historical struggles, rather than making those waging these struggles invisible under a pervasive stereotype. It is not up to

Western women to diagnose inequality in Arab society—it has been diagnosed. Rather, American women should recognize that Arab women themselves—and even some Arab men— have grappled with gender inequality for over a century. This is the message that American feminists have largely not heard, although it must be heard and Arab women's voices included in the discussion of building bridges and confronting women's issues on a global scale.

Periodical Bibliography

The following articles have been selected to supplement the diverse views presented in this chapter.

Ruth Abbey	"Back Toward a Comprehensive Liberalism?" *Political Theory*, February 2007.
Alison Bartlett	"Twenty-first Century Feminisms," *Australian Feminist Studies*, March 2007.
Kira Cochrane	"A Good Year for the F-word," *New Statesman*, January 1, 2007.
Carol Anne Douglas	"The Death of Feminism," *Off Our Backs*, Spring 2006.
Helen Graham	"Post-pleasure," *Feminist Media Studies*, March 2007.
Catherine Hakim	"Dancing with the Devil? Essentialism and Other Feminist Heresies," *British Journal of Sociology*, March 2007.
Laura A. Hebert	"Taking 'Difference' Seriously: Feminisms and the 'Man Question,'" *Journal of Gender Studies*, March 2007.
Renée M. LaReau	"Redesigning Women," *U.S. Catholic*, January 2007.
Harvey C. Mansfield	"A New Feminism," *Society*, January–February 2007.
Toril Moi	"'I Am Not a Feminist, But . . .': How Feminism Became the F-Word," *PMLA: Publications of the Modern Language Association of America*, October 2006.
Heather A. Oesterreich	"From 'Crisis' to 'Activist': The Everyday Freedom Legacy of Black Feminisms," *Race, Ethnicity & Education*, March 2007.
Naomi Schaefer Riley	"What Happens After the Revolution?" *Wall Street Journal*, December 15, 2006.

CHAPTER 2

How Has Feminism Impacted Female Sexuality and Reproduction?

Chapter Preface

A lmost immediately after the 1973 *Roe vs. Wade* ruling, the controversial Supreme Court case that made it legal for women to have abortions up to the third month, people have both feared and encouraged its possible overthrow. Few moments in recent history have spawned so much controversy among men and women, and people are often surprised to learn that not all feminists support a woman's right to have an abortion. In the early 2000s, the abortion debate has been focused on the rights of underage girls to have abortions without parental consent.

As of 2007, only six states do not require parental consent before an underage girl can have an abortion. Susan Lloyd Yolen, vice president, Public Affairs and Communication, Planned Parenthood of Connecticut, one of those six states, argues that maintaining doctor-patient confidentiality in the case of underage abortions is essential to the well-being of the young women involved. She asserts, "Assurances of confidentiality increase the number of teens willing to disclose sensitive health information to health care providers and commit to return for future health care visits." Other women have argued that by requiring parental consent, the rights of these girls are being threatened, and they may not get the abortion in time or at all.

However, some proponents of parental consent have argued that by allowing such abortions, sexual predators will never get caught and the best interests of underage girls will not be served. Given that in most states sex with underaged individuals is against the law, erasing one of the most visible signs of such a crime, pregnancy, through abortion will allow sexual predators to go unpunished. Furthermore, many supporters of parental consent laws have argued that underage girls do not have the right to make the decision for themselves, given that any other major medical procedures requires parental permission. *North County Times* staff writer, Jim Trageser, argues that "when faced with such a serious, perhaps overwhelming decision, minors need the guidance of the adults who have been legally entrusted with their welfare."

It is clear that no matter which way the law turns in regards to underage girls, abortion, and parental consent, many girls will continue to face this decision. Although teen pregnancy rates declined substantially in the last few decades of the twentieth century, the Centers for Disease Control and Prevention reports that thousands of girls aged 15–17 get pregnant each year. As the authors in the following chapter argue, much is at stake for women when it comes to sexuality and reproductive rights. In the end, education and support may be the best tools for helping young women navigate these conflicting issues.

"I oppose pornography and prostitution because I do not believe selling women and girls for sex can ever be positive or empowering."

Pornography Is Harmful to Women

Stephanie Cleveland

In the following viewpoint Stephanie Cleveland, poet and national spokeswoman for the abolition of pornography and prostitution, states that pornography has no value in a society that favors the fair and equal treatment of women. She argues that all pornography dehumanizes women and debases sex. Furthermore, she asserts that even if the industry were run by women for women, the end result would be the same—the exploitation of women solely for the sexual gratification of others. Rather than offering choices for sexual expression, pornography limits choices by imposing ideas about what sex can and should be.

As you read, consider the following questions:

1. How much yearly profit does the pornography industry make?

Stephanie Cleveland, "Hot Cherry Pies: Pornography and Justice for Women," *www.adonismirror.com*, January 16, 2006. Reproduced by permission.

2. How old is the average American boy the first time he sees pornography?

3. What percentage of the pornography industry's content is produced by women?

A few weeks ago, I attended a Take Back the Night rally on my college campus. The evening was devoted to raising awareness about rape. I was glad to be there, glad to be supporting an event that criticized men's violence against women, and glad to be surrounded by some incredible women, many of whom were survivors of sexual assault. But even though I felt proud to be taking part, I also felt sad. As I listened to the speakers who had been chosen to address our group, I heard discussion of everything from date rape, to harmful depictions of women on television, but there was one issue nobody seemed willing to talk about. No one said anything about pornography.

No one spoke about the fact that the women in pornography and prostitution are survivors, too. No one mentioned that over two thirds of women in pornography experience childhood sex abuse before entering the industry. Nobody talked about how frequently prostituted women are raped, beaten and murdered, and no one questioned whether or not there might be similarities between the descriptions given by some women in pornography, of how filming a scene feels, ("It's like I'm outside of myself, like I'm watching what's happening to me"), and the dissociation rape victims sometimes talk about experiencing. While everybody acknowledged that we live in a culture where men often feel they have the right to take sex by force, no one seemed willing to admit most men also feel they have a right to buy it. No one brought up the issue of pornography except me. As a feminist, I brought it up. I oppose pornography and prostitution because I do not believe selling women and girls for sex can ever be positive or empowering. To me, standing in opposition to pornography and prostitution seems like the only truly progressive position to take. But I was amazed at the lack of support I got at the rally. And I am constantly amazed at how hated criticism of pornography seems to be.

Pornography Dehumanizes Women

I oppose pornography and prostitution because they hurt women, including me. As a woman, I would like to be treated as an equal human being. I would like equal treatment for all women, but I do not see how we can reach that goal, as long as some of us can be bought and sold for men to use. Not surprisingly, my feelings about pornography do not make me popular with men. I can count on one hand the number of male friends I have had who supported my work against pornography. I am not conservative, at all. I am strongly pro-choice, pro-environment, anti-marriage, anti-capitalist, and extremely supportive of lesbian and gay rights. Most of the men I speak to about pornography agree with me on these issues. They identify themselves as liberal, and feel that the subordination of human beings is wrong. They believe that massive corporations do not have the right to exploit people in the name of global capitalism—unless those corporations are part of the pornography industry.

The sex industry, however, is founded on capitalism, greed, and men's contempt for women and people of color. It frequently defines sex as a service women perform for men, and it almost exclusively markets women's bodies, usually photographed in submissive positions, to men and even boys. It sexualizes racist stereotypes about Black women, Asian women and other women of color, and promotes racist beliefs about men of color as well. Yet, most of the liberal men I know defend their right to use pornography despite their supposed commitment to social justice. They defend pornography despite the fact that, in the most popular pornography, women's humiliation and subordination are eroticized. . . . A glance around a typical store that sells pornography, one glance at the DVDs and magazines that line the shelves, will tell you, I am describing mainstream pornography, not examples that are extreme or on the margins.

Pornography features violence, racism, and sexism, passed off as speech, but pornography is neither speech nor fantasy. Pornography is made by doing real things to real women. Many women might choose *not* to work in the pornography industry, if they were not physically or mentally coerced. Women might make different choices, if we did not grow up learning to base so much of our self-worth on whether or not men find us sexually attractive. Oftentimes, women experience having our boundaries broken down by men very early, when we are still children, through incest and other forms of abuse. Women are also poor, relative to men, and when women live in poverty, we do what is needed to survive, or to help our children survive, even if that includes selling sex. A lot can happen to women in a male dominated culture that still teaches us sex is our greatest power, that the most valuable thing we have to offer men is letting them f——us. People who defend pornography do not consider that these factors, rooted in sexism, do influence women to enter the industry, and might be influencing them to stay, even when they are harmed.

Often liberal men and some women remind me that pornography is not the only problem facing women. They suggest I focus my energies on more important issues. The first male friend I tried to talk to about how pornography made me feel, told me I should focus my efforts on sexist depictions of women in what he described as, other, more mainstreamed media. The pornography industry has an over 10 billion dollar a year profit margin. It is as mainstreamed as television commercials, sitcoms, or any other media that might promote sexist stereotypes about women, and pornography often infiltrates those media as well. The average boy growing up in

America will see pornography for the first time when he is eleven years old. Pornography begins extremely early, to fuse men's desire with the treatment of women as less than human, in a way TV commercials do not. Men learn to orgasm to images of women they use in pornography. Through pornography, men learn to use women for sexual release, and then put us away. At best, pornography connects male sexual pleasure with the belief men have the right to buy sexual access to women; at worst, it allows men to climax to images of women's suffering.

Dominating Women

Most men and women I know who use pornography believe sex is about power differences. They feel domination, submission and gender are inherent and natural parts of sex. Any critique of sadomasochism, they suggest, is puritanical—the rougher the sex filmed in pornography, the realer it must be, since, according to them, male sexuality is naturally coercive, female sexuality naturally masochistic. Anyone who thinks sex could and should be about tenderness, caring or respect, is fooling herself, (or himself) being naïve, judgmental. Yet, pornography is offering its own judgments about what sex between men and women should be. . . .

For defenders of pornography, violence against women is natural, at least within the context of the industry. It cannot be called abuse, because the women get paid. Violence in pornography does not matter because women consent, if we are given money. The underlying assumption is, that some women (if not all) enjoy being used. What does that say about women's status in the twenty-first century, about men's view of women in general? One man, a poet and editor, who defended his pornography use to me explained simply, "women like to be dominated." I think that is an attitude a lot of men who use pornography hold. Women who question pornography are told we aren't looking at it the right way. . . . We are told not to consider whether or not her free choice really hurts, whether it hurts her dignity as a person, having other men watch her being used, having men bond together over the collective use of her body; whether it hurts women exposed to pornography made of her later, by men in their own lives; whether it hurts women as a class, in and outside the industry.

The majority of women who go into pornography are poor. They have fewer privileges in life, generally speaking, than men and women who defend pornography, and men who use them. A lot of women in pornography and prostitution did not get to go to college like me. Yet, as a feminist, if I show concern for women in pornography, I am sometimes accused of denying them agency. While liberal men and women agree that people living in poverty are entitled to help and compassion, that being poor does not mean you are stupid or less entitled to human dignity—for some reason, there is this assumption that women being sold through pornography do not deserve to leave, that women should not be encouraged to know they deserve better out of life. Some tell me I am *anti-feminist* if I suggest that all women deserve better than being marketed as, what one prostitution survivor termed, spittoons for men's semen. I am making women into victims, if I say pornography hurts them, hurts me. Yet, the only freedom I truly want to take away is the freedom men have to buy sexual access to women. Women in pornography should be unionized and well-vetted, its defenders repeat, but never, ever encouraged to leave.

But what would happen if the women did leave? What would happen to men, if women in pornography decided to leave, if they actually could? Would men die without pornography? Are men really so hooked on the misogyny pornography sells, that they can no longer live without it?

Dworkin and MacKinnon's Definition of Pornography

In the early 1980s, feminist writer Andrea Dworkin and lawyer Catharine MacKinnon joined forces to develop anti-pornography legislation. In order to do so, they had to develop a clear definition of pornography:

Pornography is the graphic sexually explicit subordination of women through pictures and/or words that also includes one or more of the following: (i) women are presented dehumanized as sexual objects, things or commodities; or (ii) women are presented as sexual objects who enjoy pain or humiliation; or (iii) women are presented as sexual objects who experience sexual pleasure in being raped; or (iv) women are presented as sexual objects tied up or cut up or mutilated or bruised or physically hurt; or (v) women are presented in postures or positions of sexual submission, servility, or display; or (vi) women's body parts—including but not limited to vaginas, breasts, or buttocks—are exhibited such that women are reduced to those parts; or (vii) women are presented as whores by nature; or (viii) women are presented being penetrated by objects or animals; or (ix) woman are presented in scenarios of degradation, injury, torture, shown as filthy or inferior, bleeding, bruised, or hurt in a context that makes these conditions sexual.

Dworkin and MacKinnon's now famous and widely critiqued definition was used in an ordinance passed in Indianapolis in 1984 that was later overturned as unconstitutional.

Indianapolis and Marion County, Ind.,
Code Ch. 16, § 16-3(q), 1984.

Women Controlling the Industry

It has also been suggested to me by liberal men and some women, that rather than attack pornography, I should work towards putting control of the industry into women's hands. The people who suggest this seem to believe even though patriarchy is still firmly in place, that somehow, where sex is concerned, women are able to make decisions out of freedom and equality. But women are forced to make choices about sex, and about entering into pornography, like all the other choices we make in our lives—under a system of male dominance we still are not free from. We do not control any industry on this planet, as women. It is absurd to think we do or will ever control men's pornography use. Men have the money and power to control what type of pornography gets made, and by whom. And judging from the direction the industry has taken in the past decade, men who use pornography want very much to be able to use women—they want to be able to use us without having to worry about being gentle, or feminist.

One male reviewer's comments on female pornographer Candida Royalle's website seem telling: "Not too much for my wife, but still arousing. I am not sure if it would be great to sit down to alone. I might want something a little less 'lovable.'" Women can waste time and energy making pornography that is arguably less overtly degrading, but men still have the final say over what pornography they'll use. Sadly, women, like men, can abuse other people, and women, like men, can become pimps. This is why the idea of a woman-run pornography industry is not only unlikely, but terribly sad. In that case, the industry would still be based on injustice—on the selling of some people as sex, on women catering to men, giving men what men want, rather than asking them for social change—the only difference would be, women would be the pimps as well as the victims.

The lives of women hurt by pornography should matter. The lives of those who feel broken by pornography should matter, too, more than any inherently compromised attempts to rework the industry. Why is it so unacceptable to ask men to give up pornography? The speech of those raped by pornography users, and by men who pressure and force women to act out scenes from pornography—should be allowed to matter. Their voices should matter more than the speech rights of men, who *can* live without pornography. Women hurt in pornography should also count more than the voices of a small, elite group of women willing to defend pornography. These women exploit other women, in order to make money. Women who claim pornography empowers us all, operate from a position of privilege. They do not have to live through being assaulted by a father who uses pornography, or being bullied into performing sex acts by boyfriends who use it. This tiny group of women pornographers gets to stand behind the camera, producing about one percent of the industry's content. Men, and especially men who make pornography, are only too happy to support them. . . .

Not About Woman's Sexuality

Pro-pornography women claim they are entitled to their individual freedom of expression (how free one can be to express ideas about women and sex, within a form men invented, is hard to understand). Feminism should be about giving women choices as individuals, they say. And that's true, to some extent, but it's also true that feminism is about resisting male dominance, that the most important goal of feminism is doing what is best for the status of women as a group. Women who identify as feminists have a responsibility to think about how our choices and public statements as women, can affect other women's lives. As a woman who was harmed by repeated exposure to pornography in her childhood, I can honestly say that my father's pornography would have been just as hurtful to me, whether a man or woman made it. Some women may learn to enjoy pornography, but many more have been hurt in and through it. Some women may try to see sex as power, but many more realize power is still in the hands of men, whenever they decide whom they will buy sexual access to. Why should women be expected to reclaim an industry men came up with to begin with? Why should we try to make lovable pornography, working within the same system of patriarchy and capitalism men continue to run? Couldn't we use our energy to create our own ideas about sex instead, ideas that do not involve pornography at all? . . .

The problem is, pornography is not about women's sexuality at all—those aspects of sex that are valuable, that involve knowing and connecting with another person as a human, cannot be shown in pornography; Pornography is a substitute for intimacy, a sexist one, for relating to women through sex. But sex with women cannot be commercially boxed and marketed, precisely because it is human, because women are.

Some women, and maybe even some men, would like to experience sex that is not commercial. Some of us are 'pro-sex,' to the point of wanting sex as human beings. . . .

I have my own appetites; I do not need the sexual script that pornographers—male or female—want to sell me. I have my own ambitions. I want the chance to find my own vision of sex. I want lovers who are willing to abandon pornography, so that I can have partners in respect and equality. . . .

> *"We do not believe that sexually explicit photos and words are intrinsically exploitative, degrading, or objectifying."*

Pornography Is Not Harmful to Women

Barbara Dority

Barbara Dority is executive director of the Washington Coalition Against Censorship (WCAC) and is founder/co-chair of the Northwest Feminists Anti-Censorship Taskforce (NW-FACT). In the following viewpoint she argues that censorship of any material, including pornography, goes against the founding principles of feminism. She asserts that contrary to most anti-pornography beliefs, pornography rarely exploits or enacts violence against women. In addition, Dority notes that the assertion that pornography leads to sexism is untrue. Ultimately, censoring pornography, censors women's rights to freedom of expression.

As you read, consider the following questions:

1. According to the author, what are the two crucial issues involved in the debate about pornography and women?
2. The author states that studies have found that approximately what percentage of all pornographic materials contains violent or coercive images?

Barbara Dority, "Feminist Moralism, Pornography, and Censorship," *http:// privat.ub.uib.no/bubsy/dority.htm*. Reproduced by permission.

3. According to the author, what percentage of all porno-graphic media present women as active sexual agents?

The First Amendment does not say there is to be freedom of speech and press provided it is not sexually explicit, or considered dangerous or offensive by anyone. The authors of the Bill of Rights had learned firsthand why it was absolutely necessary to permit all manner of ideas to be expressed in the new Republic. They had lived under repressive governments, ruled absolutely by the majority. After careful consideration and debate, they concluded that the guarantees of free speech and press could not be confined to the expression of ideas that are conventional or shared by the majority, but must also always extend to those ideas considered—by the many or by the few—to be socially undesirable or even repugnant. They gave us a precious legacy based upon the firm conviction that the only way for all citizens to be truly free was to permit all expression and to accept and deal with the inherent risks. The strength and beauty of the First Amendment is that it protects whatever images and words we hate as well as those we cherish. . . .

Feminism itself could not exist without these guarantees. It is only because of the First Amendment in the United States and its equivalents in other countries that women have been able to speak and write in favor of reproductive freedom and gender equality. History shows that censorship and suppres-sion work directly against feminist goals and are often used to limit women's rights in the name of protection. Feminists should remember that efforts were made to silence women who first spoke on the subject of birth control on the grounds that the subject was obscene. Margaret Sanger was jailed for attempting to set up birth control clinics and her publication, *Woman Rebel*, was suppressed and confiscated—all on the grounds of obscenity. Censorship and suppression of any kind are in direct conflict with feminist principles of freedom and tolerance. Of all people, feminists should be the most outspoken and staunch defenders of the First Amendment—because feminism and civil liberties are, by definition, totally inextricable.

The issue of pornography versus both feminism and the First Amendment has engendered an intense debate—a debate which directly involves a great many issues. Will feminism continue to capitulate to self-righteous moralism and to perpetuate blatant and vicious sexism, or will it wake up and take a stand for the liberation of women in all domains, including the difficult and often contradictory domain of sexual expression, which must, of necessity, involve the liberation of men as well? . . .

There are two crucial issues involved in this debate. First, the moralistic condemnations of pornography and male sexuality, indeed, maleness itself, by so-called feminists, and, second, the translation of that condemnation by nearly all contemporary feminist leaders and writers into calls for various kinds of legislation which would effectively ban pornographic imagery and words, including adult entertainment. Both of these campaigns are very alarming to many of us.

The concept of anti-pornography ordinances is based upon the notion that pornography is a civil rights issue because it degrades women and encourages discrimination against them. Feminists maintain that pornography is sex discrimination and 'hate literature' against women—a legal violation of women's civil rights. . . .

This civil rights violation approach runs contrary to all existing civil rights laws, the intent and application of which clearly establish that, legally, discrimination is not what people say, or write, or depict about other people—discrimination is what people do to other people. Any method which attacks pictures or words with certain themes is fundamentally at odds with the entire civil rights approach used in most countries to combat discrimination and oppression. Conduct is the subject of all civil rights legislation. In a free society, there are no crimes of thought—only crimes of action.

The claim that certain forms of expression are dangerous and an incitement to violence has been used time after time to try to prohibit speech that some people don't like. Although some of us do not support exceptions to the First Amendment, believing there are other equally effective ways to deal with any problems, the notion of 'a clear and present danger' was formulated by the United States Supreme Court to address this threat. I refer to the concept commonly called 'yelling 'Fire!' in a crowded theatre.' It is currently against the law in the United States to exercise one's right of free speech in this manner because it is said to present a clear and immediate danger to others since injuries are possible in the panic to escape, and there would be no time for 'counteracting speech' before such a reaction set in.

For pornography to be suppressed under this test, we would have to demonstrate that any viewer is likely to be provoked to sexual violence immediately upon seeing it. Even most anti-pornography crusaders do not claim that this is true. . . .

The assertion that pornography leads to sexism and violence forms the basis for these proposals. This totally unsupported claim draws on simplistic behaviorist psychology and has been repeatedly discredited by reputable specialists in sexual behavior. Even the notorious Meese Commission on pornography (which was stacked with conservative, anti-porn activists) reported that no such causal link can be substantiated. [The Meese Commission is the nickname given to the Attorney General's Commission on Pornography, which was convened in 1986 by U.S. Attorney General Edwin Meese. The 1,960-page report has been severely criticized by many opponents and supported widely by others.] Many studies show no effects from the viewing of sexually explicit materials, whether violent or not, and some studies suggest that exposure to por-

A Pro-Sex Defense of Pornography

As a "pro-sex" feminist, I contend: Pornography benefits women, both personally and politically. . . .

Pornography breaks cultural and political stereotypes, so that each woman can interpret sex for herself. Anti-feminists tell women to be ashamed of their appetites and urges. Pornography tells them to accept and enjoy them. . . .

Pornography benefits women politically in many ways. Historically, pornography and feminism have been fellow travelers and natural allies. Although it is not possible to draw a cause-and-effect relationship between the rise of pornography and that of feminism, they both demand the same social conditions—namely, sexual freedom.

Pornography is free speech applied to the sexual realm. Freedom of speech is the ally of those who seek change: it is the enemy of those who seek to maintain control. Pornography, along with all other forms of sexual heresy, such as homosexuality, should have the same legal protection as political heresy. This protection is especially important to women, whose sexuality has been controlled by censorship through the centuries.

Viewing pornography may well have a cathartic effect on men who have violent urges toward women. If this is true, restricting pornography removes a protective barrier between women and abuse. . . .

Wendy McElroy, "A Feminist Defense of Pornography,"
Free Inquiry, vol. 17, no. 4, Fall 1997.

nography may be beneficial by serving as an outlet for persons who might otherwise offend. In point of fact, evidence indicates that sexual offenders are typically raised in sexually repressed homes and have had less exposure to sexually explicit materials than non-offenders. Many of us believe that a large portion of the real answer to reducing violence, especially sexual violence, lies in more speech and in more openness about sexuality.

Studies of the content of men's magazines and adult videos have found that violent or coercive imagery is a very small fraction of all sexual images—approximately 5%—and that there is much less violence in pornography than in nonsexual media. There is far more violence in Saturday morning cartoons than in 95% of all sexually explicit media. Even the strongest advocates of censorship must usually admit that most men can look at a 'men's magazine' without being overcome by uncontrollable urges to assault women and children.

Anecdotal stories of sex offenders who are found to possess pornography are often cited. As [sex educator and clinical Psychologist] Sol Gordon has pointed out, a large percentage of these offenders are also found to possess milk in their refrigerators. Sporadic incidents do not prove a correlation, nor does a correlation prove causation. This is a basic maxim of any scientific research, and holds particularly true when attempting to examine and predict the complexities of human behavior.

Another point which must be made is that if these proposed censorship laws are passed, an illusion would be created that something is being done to end sexism and sexual violence, an illusion that would have a harmful effect in and of itself. We need, all of us, to address the problems of violence in our societies—violence to both women and men and to male and female children. But these censorship measures now being promoted by alliances of feminists and conservatives will be counterproductive and worthless.

Sexism and violence toward women, and men, was a reality long before pornography as we know it today existed and long before there were facilities for the mass distribution of words and images. Sexist and violent materials are symptoms of a sexist and violent society—not the causes. Sexist and violent materials do not create violence, people do. If we really want to address violence, the movement against pornography is a diversion. Pornography is not violence. Stopping it will not stop violence. In point of fact, we have a good deal of evidence to indicate that such a further regression into sexual suppression would serve to significantly increase violence.

Even if it is assumed that a small percentage of people are 'encouraged' to engage in sexist behavior or commit violent acts after exposure to certain books or films, this still would not justify suppression. Such a 'pervert's veto' would threaten a broad range of literature and film. Should we allow the unstable few to exercise a veto over what the rest of us may hear, see, or read? A free society must accept the risks that come with liberty. . . .

In many repressive countries—whether in Central America, Asia, Africa, Eastern Europe, or the Middle East, there is practically no pornography, but there is a great deal of sexism and violence against women—and men. In the Netherlands and Scandinavia, where there are almost no restrictions on sexually explicit materials, the rate of sex-related crime is much lower than in the United States. Pornography is virtually irrelevant to the existence of sexism and violence. Again, Sol Gordon says, 'The elimination of sexually explicit material would not prevent one single rape.' Only the arduous process of education, the transformation of hearts and minds, will change the manifestations of sexism and violence in our culture and in our world—sexism and violence against women, children, and men.

Nor does a causal relationship exist between an increase in the availability of pornography and inequality for women. While pornography and the availability thereof has increased over the past 50 years, the rights of women have jumped dramatically. If a correlation existed, couldn't we expect the opposite to be true? Shall we conclude, then, that the increased availability of pornography has been directly responsible for the advancement of women's rights? Obviously, both these assertions of causal relationships are spurious. . . .

Many feminists would have us believe that all pornography is violent. But, in reality, as we have already seen, a very small percentage of sexually explicit material can be said to contain images of violence or coercion. In 95% of all pornographic media, women are presented as active agents of their own powerful sexuality and shown as experiencing as much pleasure as men. In the fantasy-land of pornography, sex is guilt-free, not connected with reproduction or tied to monogamy or marriage, and enjoyed equally by male and female. It is difficult to see why such portrayals are sexist or demeaning to women—or to men. Unless, of course, common heterosexual activities in and of themselves are assumed to be demeaning to women. And here lies the answer. Many 'feminist scholars and theorists' bluntly maintain that heterosexual sex itself is inherently degrading to women and is always, in actuality, rape. . . .

Nevertheless, the five percent of pornography which can be said to contain images of violence or coercion is worthy of our consideration. 'Violent pornography' is viewed by many as the most offensive form of expression. Most of this material consists of what is commonly called sadomasochistic images and words and can be seen in two ways: as the depiction of consensual sadomasochism or as the depiction of actual coercion and violence against non-consenting persons. If it is the latter, the actual perpetrators of the violence or coercion have broken the law and should be prosecuted to its full extent. However, not everyone sees the degradation of women or men in depictions of 'violent' sexual activity. What some find degrading, others find erotic. . . .

But we are told by most feminists that we must especially condemn not only all materials depicting violence but the sexual practices associated with S & M themselves to prove that we are opposed to violence against women. We must condemn nearly all sexually explicit materials as degrading to women and label pornography a principal cause of women's oppression in order to retain our credentials as feminists. Many feminist women and men refuse to do this. We believe it is possible to be feminists dedicated to equal rights and the elimination of violence against women while defending the freedom of all kinds of sexual expression. We believe that our work against violence must be directed at actual instances of violence against both men and women, rather than at images in sex magazines and videos.

'Pornography is violence against women'—a popular organizing slogan in both the United States and Canada. Come on—let's get real. It is abundantly clear that the real locus of the anti-pornograpny campaign is not violence, but sex and images of sexual behavior. I believe that sexual materials are being attacked because sex has always been an easy, vulnerable target and has always been something from which our cultures have 'protected' women. Most of us still live in extremely sexually inhibited societies. . . .

I, along with many other feminists, do not believe that *Playboy* and *Penthouse* are sexist or that the presentation of the naked female body, whether or not in 'inviting positions,' [is] intrinsically sexist. We do not believe that sexually explicit photos and words are intrinsically exploitative, degrading, or objectifying. . . .

Many of us, women and men, do not accept the assertion that women presented as active agents of their own sexuality are 'on display' and 'dehumanized as sexual objects,' or that women represented as engaging in sex with more than one man are being pictured as 'whores by nature.' These moralistic ideologies alienate not only women in the sex industry, but also women who create their own sexual pleasure without regard for its political correctness. Many of us believe it is a tragedy that the feminist movement has been drawn into an anti-sex stance, condemning 'deviant' sexual representation and expression as part of a moralistic tangent to wipe out smut. . . .

It is argued that women who work in the adult entertainment industry are often abused. Yes, this is too often true. We should be working to see that those who perpetrate this abuse are arrested and prosecuted to the full extent of the law. These women receive less protection and are sometimes abused specifically because the larger community has stigmatized them, condemning them as 'bad women,' including their feminist 'sisters.' We should be working for the rights and safety of these women and promoting respect for them and their work, not further jeopardizing them by heaping scorn on their work and attempting to criminalize it.

As for women who enjoy pornography—feminists have pronounced them 'brainwashed by patriarchy.' This Victorian imagery—pure, morally superior women controlling the vile, lustful impulses of men and being unable to think independently for themselves—is a sexist stereotype we should be working against, not one we should be promoting. In this analysis, as many 'feminist theorists' bluntly tell us, women can never freely choose to have sex with men. In this analysis, women can never choose to use 'male-identified' imagery in their sexual fantasies and practices and certainly can't ever freely choose to earn their living by inviting the rapacious male gaze or providing sexual services to men.

Tragically, all the various aspects of this anti-male and anti-pornography campaign are diverting funds and energy from work that will diminish sexism and violence. Abortion rights are under seige in the U.S., and, despite constant agitation by some of us, there has been no serious or concerted effort to reintroduce the Equal Rights Amendment. Advocacy and work toward job training, quality day and health care; access to birth control, accurate sex education and the teaching of critical thinking skills in schools; and funding for battered women's shelters and rape crisis centers must be undertaken. . . .

Many of us believe that all this feminist moralizing and sexism against men and its attendant calls for censorship have totally undermined the integrity of the feminist movement. Being a feminist means being against sexism, not against sex. . . .

Many of us, women and men, insist on the right to choose both freedom and sexuality. We cannot afford to remain divided and sidetracked. Let us, men and women, create a movement for real gender equality and the elimination of violence against all people. Only by working for meaningful social reform can we ever hope to live in the safe, just society of our dreams. . . .

*"Women need to have the right and free-
dom to choose how to live their lives as
sexual beings. This includes prostitution."*

Women Have the Right
to be Prostitutes

Kimberly Klinger

*In the following viewpoint Kimberly Klinger, a freelance writer
who focuses on race, gender, and class issues, argues that women
have the right to be prostitutes. She believes that prostitutes and
the women who support their rights can and often are feminists.
Furthermore, Klinger asserts that legalizing, or at the very least
decriminalizing, prostitution will benefit women and society as a
whole by regulating industry practices and keeping the choice to
sell sex available to all women.*

As you read, consider the following questions:

1. In what year did Dworkin and MacKinnon write anti-
   pornography bills?
2. What are the five tenets of decriminalizing prostitution
   as set forth by the World Charter for Prostitute Rights
   in 1985?

Kimberly Klinger, "Prostitution, Humanism, and a Woman's Choice: Perspectives on
Prostitution," *Humanist*, January–February 2003. Copyright © 2003 American Humanist
Association. Reproduced by permission of the author.

3. Name three groups that advocate for the rights of sex workers.

Driving home in the early morning hours after a night out in Washington, D.C., I turn from 14th to L Street near downtown. I'm only on the street for a block before I hit the clogged artery of Massachusetts Avenue, and this particular area seems devoid of important business or commerce. Except for the prostitutes.

Almost every weekend night I can spot women walking up and down the street—sometimes between the cars and quite near to my own. They're stereotypically wearing the tiniest slivers of fabric masquerading as dresses, swishing their hips as they teeter on high heels. I don't recall ever seeing any possible pimps nearby and wonder if these women operate independently. I wonder about a lot of things, actually. Are they happy? Are they safe? Are they making good money? Are they feminists?

Fighting Stereotypes

That last question may seem incongruous, but to me it's relevant. As a third wave feminist, I find sex and sex work to be important issues—ones which are being addressed in ways unheard of by our foremothers. We third wavers are, in many cases, the lip-gloss wearing, *BUST* magazine reading, pro-sex women of the new millennium. We have taken the liberties of the second wave and run with them, demanding even more freedom as we struggle to find our new identities in the ever-dominating patriarchy. We don't hold consciousness-raising sessions; we hold safe sex fairs. We still march on Washington, but we have punk rock bands helping us to raise the funds to get there. We're more multicultural and diverse, yet we continue to fight the white face—the opinion that feminism is a white women's movement—put upon us by the media.

We've also had to fight the awful stereotype that feminists are frigid, man-hating, anti-sex zealots. The second wave made incredible changes in how the United States deals with rape and domestic violence, and while we still have a long way to go, these issues are at least taken much more seriously. However, in the process, feminists have been labeled and demonized, thus creating a huge chasm between sexuality and feminism. Women are still the same sexual beings they always were, but to outsiders they have been considered strictly buzz-kills (no fun) or—gasp—lesbians. In 1983 Andrea Dworkin and Catharine A. MacKinnon wrote major antipornography bills that negatively labeled feminists as anti-sex instead of pro-human rights.

In the third wave, pornography, sex, and prostitution aren't presented as black and white issues. For instance, pornography isn't simply seen as degrading sexual imagery made by men, for men. There are female filmmakers and feminist porn stars who want to reclaim their right to enjoy sexual images without violence and negativity. Sex is more widely discussed than ever and taboos are being broken every day. The third wave hopes to expand definitions of sexuality. For women to be liberated sexually, they must be able to live as they choose, to break out of narrow ideas of sexuality, to be sexual and still be respected, and essentially to be whole. Feminism and sex work aren't therefore mutually exclusive. Choice is key here—women need to have the right and freedom to choose how to live their lives as sexual beings. This includes prostitution.

In Support of Safe Prostitution

Prostitution. The word normally calls to mind women down on their luck, pitied cases who walk the streets at night with little protection or rights—essentially women who have no other choice. And unfortunately this often isn't far from the truth. In the United States and worldwide many women turn to or are forced into sexual prostitution because they have limited options. But there are other situations, even in the United States, where women turn to this profession and other sex work because they want to. They are fortunate to have real choices and select this path because it suits them, while practicing prostitution safely and respectfully.

In the United States it is possible to find a number of organizations of sex workers who defend each other, work alongside international groups to decriminalize prostitution and protect prostitutes, and share the common experiences of choosing and enjoying this form of labor. There are advocacy and rights organizations, international conferences, and famous porn stars who all regard prostitution and other sex work as just that: a job and a way to earn a living. They argue that it should be treated as such—protected under the law with safety guidelines, unions, networks, and all the rest. Furthermore, taking a third wave feminist view, they maintain that women need to have the right and freedom to choose how to live their lives as sexual beings, including taking up "the world's oldest profession."

No matter what wave of feminism is applied, all feminists agree that forced, coerced, poverty-based, trafficked, and unprotected prostitution should be opposed. In countries where prostitution is illegal, such as in forty-nine of fifty states in the United States, women have no protection, socially or legally. The situation is messy at best and, at worst, violent, dangerous, and all but devoid of human rights. For example, most American prostitutes have to work for pimps or out of brothels, never seeing much of the money they have earned. If they are streetwalkers they live in fear of criminal assault or arrest—and in some cases, sexual abuse by police. They may be forced to deal with customers they are afraid of or who harm them. If they are raped, police will generally disregard their suffering, not even considering what in any other profession would be recognized as criminal assault and the forced rendering of service without pay. Beyond that, the victimized woman may even be arrested for practicing prostitution. The situation is even worse in poor countries where it is all too common for young girls to be forced into prostitution and where men from wealthier nations travel specifically to have sex with them.

Second wave feminist author MacKinnon has essentially deemed prostitution sexual slavery, arguing that the relevant laws immensely harm women, classifying them as criminals and denying them their basic civil rights. MacKinnon admits in an essay, "Prostitution and Civil Rights" published in the *Michigan Journal of Gender and Law* (1993) that she isn't sure about what to do legally concerning prostitution but that international initiatives and policy responses can help to put the power back in women's hands where it belongs. Does this mean all prostitution would disappear if women had their say? Not if the numerous prostitute rights groups and their sympathizers are any indication.

Decriminalizing Prostitution

For many who have thought about this question, dismissing the entire sex industry as abusive and immoral only exacerbates existing problems and tosses the concerns of sex workers aside. Therefore many feminists, civil rights workers, and human rights activists argue for the decriminalization—not necessarily the legalization—of prostitution. Internationally, conferences are held that address decriminalization. The World Charter for Prostitutes Rights is one outcome. Created in 1985 this document is a template used by human rights groups all over the world—it makes certain basic demands abundantly clear:

1. Decriminalize all aspects of adult prostitution resulting from individual decision. This includes regulation of third parties (business managers) according to standard business codes.

2. Strongly enforce all laws against fraud, coercion, violence, child sexual abuse, child labor, rape, and racism everywhere and across national boundaries, whether or not in the context of prostitution.

Legalization and Decriminalization Defined

Legalization

From a sociological perspective, the term legalization usually refers to a system of criminal regulation and government control of prostitutes, wherein certain prostitutes are given licenses which permit them to work in specific and usually limited ways. Although legalization can also imply a decriminalized, autonomous system of prostitution, in reality, in most "legalized" systems the police have relegated the job of prostitution control through criminal codes. Laws regulate prostitutes' businesses and lives, prescribing health checks and registration of health status . . . , telling prostitutes where they may or may not reside, prescribing full time employment for their lovers, etc. . . .

Decriminalization

Prostitutes' rights organizations (ie, COYOTE, National Task Force on Prostitution) use the term decriminalization to mean the removal of laws against prostitution. Decriminalization is usually used to refer to total decriminalization, that is, the repeal of laws against consensual adult sexual activity, in commercial and non-commercial contexts. . . . Prostitutes' rights advocates call for decriminalization of all aspects of prostitution resulting from individual decision. Asserting the right to work as prostitutes, many claim their right to freedom of choice of management. They claim that laws against pimping (living off the earnings) are often used against domestic partners and children, and these laws serve to prevent prostitutes from organizing their businesses and working together for mutual protection. . . .

Prostitutes' Education Network, "Decriminalizing and Legalizing: Defining Terms," www.bayswan.org, 2002.

3. Guarantee prostitutes all human rights and civil liberties, including the freedom of speech, travel, immigration, work, marriage, and motherhood and the right to unemployment insurance, health insurance, and housing.
4. Ensure that prostitutes' rights are protected.
5. Allow prostitutes to unionize.

Decriminalization essentially means the removal of laws against this and other forms of sex work. The Prostitutes Education Network clarifies that decriminalization is usually used to refer to total decriminalization—that is, the repeal of all laws against consensual adult sexual activity in both commercial and noncommercial contexts. This allows the individual prostitute to choose whether or not she is managed and protects her from fraud, abuse, and coercion.

Legalizing Prostitution

By contrast the term legalization usually refers to a system of governmental regulation of prostitutes wherein prostitutes are licensed and required to work in specific ways. When Jesse Ventura was running for the Minnesota governorship in 1998 he proposed that Minnesotans should consider legalizing prostitution in order to have governmental control and keep it out of residential areas. This is the practice in Nevada, the only state in the United States where brothels are legal. Although legalization can also imply a decriminalized, autonomous system of prostitution, the reality is that in most "legalized" systems the police control prostitution with criminal codes. Laws regulate prostitutes' businesses and lives, prescribing health checks and registration of health status. According to the International Union of Sex Workers, legalized systems often include special taxes, the restriction of prostitutes to working in brothels or in certain zones, licenses, registration of prostitutes and the consequent keeping of records of each individual in the profession, and health checks which often result in punitive quarantine. This is why the World Charter for Prostitutes Rights doesn't support mandatory health checks. This may be controversial but it fits with the general idea that prostitutes' lives should be protected but not regulated. Easier and more affordable access to health clinics where prostitutes don't feel stigmatized is of greater concern to these human rights groups because compulsory checks can frighten some prostitutes and actually prevent those who are most at risk from getting necessary medical checkups. Many groups that support sex workers have sexual health and disease control as their top priorities and provide education, contraception, and health care referrals.

A well-known example of legalized prostitution is that which has been practiced in the Netherlands since the 1800s, however brothels were illegal until 2000. When the ban was lifted, forced prostitution came under harsher punishment. Brothels are now required to be licensed and it is legal to organize the prostitution of another party, provided the prostitution isn't forced. According to the A. De Graaf Foundation, laws in the Netherlands now will control and regulate the exploitation of prostitution, improve the prosecution of involuntary exploitation, protect minors, protect the position of prostitutes, combat the criminal affairs related to prostitution, and combat the presence of illegal aliens in prostitution.

Designated streetwalking zones have also been established. While these aren't without their problems, they have essentially functioned as a safe community for women to work. The zones also offer the benefit of a shelter which affords prostitutes a place to meet with their colleagues, talk to health care professionals, and generally relax. This was a good solution for an occupation that had led both police and prostitutes to feel that frequent raids were only making matters worse. Women felt scared and were always on the run, and police thought they weren't succeeding at making the streets any safer. This system of legalization seems to have worked well because in the Netherlands social attitudes about sex and sex work are more liberal than in other parts of the world. There is a genuine effort to protect and respect the rights of Dutch sex workers.

But this sort of arrangement isn't found all over the world. Nor can one say that the Netherlands example should become a model for every other country. Some societies may benefit more from decriminalization while others are decades away from any regulation whatsoever. The latter seems to be the case in the United States, where puritanical attitudes about sex in general would make it nearly impossible to treat prostitution as just another business.

Women Should Choose

What then is the best choice for women? Put simply, the best choice for women is the choice that the individual woman makes for herself. Furthermore, a humanist perspective would naturally back up the right of women to choose how to live their lives as sexual beings. Humanist Manifesto II [the 1993 update of a 1933 document that declared the necissity for global human rights,] says:

> In the area of sexuality, we believe that intolerant attitudes, often cultivated by orthodox religions and puritanical cultures, unduly repress sexual conduct. The right to birth control, abortion, and divorce should be recognized. While we do not approve of exploitive, denigrating forms of sexual expression, neither do we wish to prohibit, by law or social sanction, sexual behavior between consenting adults. The many varieties of sexual exploration should not in themselves be considered "evil." Without countenancing mindless permissiveness or unbridled promiscuity, a civilized society should be a tolerant one. Short of harming others or compelling them to do likewise, individuals should be permitted to express their sexual proclivities and pursue their lifestyles

as they desire. We wish to cultivate the development of a responsible attitude toward sexuality, in which humans are not exploited as sexual objects, and in which intimacy, sensitivity, respect, and honesty in interpersonal relations are encouraged. Moral education for children and adults is an important way of developing awareness and sexual maturity.

As stated above, any variety of sexual exploration—as long as it isn't exploitative or harmful—can't be considered evil, yet that is exactly how prostitution is regarded. If a woman or man chooses to exchange sex for money and does it in a way that causes no harm to either party, then they should be free to do so.

In this new social environment, many of the prostitutes' rights groups build from the pro-sex ideals of the third wave. Groups such as COYOTE (Call Off Your Old Tired Ethics), the Blackstockings, and PONY (Prostitutes of New York) advocate for women who have chosen to be sex workers. Their Web sites are full of resources—from legal and medical referrals to common sense safety tips—and they advocate tirelessly for the decriminalization of prostitution.

It would seem that decriminalization should be a key point in any humanistic feminist perspective on prostitution. Every woman's choices should be legally and socially respected whether a given woman chooses to be a wife, a CEO, or a prostitute.

And what is good for women in these instances becomes good for other sex workers, such as male prostitutes, exotic dancers of both sexes, and so on—this applies to both the gay and straight communities. Furthermore, what liberates those who make sex a profession also liberates everyone else who enjoys sex recreationally. General sexiness, for example, can take on more varied and open forms—so much so that no woman would need to fear that frank sexuality in manner or dress would any longer stigmatize her as a "slut" (or if it did, the word would have lost its sting).

Feminism has always advocated for women to enjoy freedom of choice. Women have made great strides in the courtrooms, the boardrooms, and the bedrooms. But there remains a long way to go. Negative attitudes toward sexuality, in particular, have made it hard for women to be fully liberated. But thanks to feminists, prostitute activists, and their supporters, things are slowly changing. Only when women have their sexual and personal choices protected and respected can they truly be free.

"Prostitution must be recognized not only as part but as a foundation of the larger system of patriarchal subordination of women."

Women Do Not Have the Right to Be Prostitutes

Coalition Against Trafficking in Women—Asia Pacific

Founded in 1988, the Coalition Against Trafficking in Women (CATW) is a non-governmental organization that promotes women's human rights by working internationally to combat sexual exploitation in all its forms. In the following viewpoint, the Asia Pacific branch of the CATW argues against prostitution in any form. They analyze and carefully rebut the most common arguments for prostitution, including the freedom of choice, the right to work, and the freedom of expression. Finally, they call on feminists to make the world a better place for women by fighting against the legalization and social acceptance of prostitution.

As you read, consider the following questions:

1. According to the authors, what two views are presented as to why women have the right to work as prostitutes?

Coalition Against Trafficking in Women—Asia Pacific, "Sex: From Intimacy to 'Sexual Labor' or Is It a Human Right to Prostitute?" http://action.web.ca/home/catw/reading room.shtml?x=16287. Reproduced by permission.

2. Rape occurs how frequently in the United States and in South Africa?

3. According to the authors, what does it mean to be pro-sex?

Debates on prostitution rage on, as they have for over a hundred years. But if the commerce of sex was once a more hidden or at least discreet business, today there's no ignoring the bombardment of sex sales talk; we live, it has been said, in a culture of pornography. With the worldwide explosion in recent decades of industries based on the production, sale and consumption of sex primarily personified in women's bodies, there is an even more pressing need to understand the commodification of sex in the range and diversity of forms that pornography, "sexual entertainment" and prostitution are taking, and for feminists to analyze the significance of and impact of these developments on women's status. . . .

Right to Self-Determination

For the pro-prostitution advocates, foremost among the human rights principles invoked to defend the right to prostitute is the right to self-determination. This is understood as the individual's right to make autonomous choices and decisions which can include engaging in consensual commercial sex as well as of setting the terms of that sexual exchange.

There are many problems with this position starting with its failure to acknowledge the social, economic and political structural imbalances and the sexual relations of power between women and men which constitute the context within which these choices and decisions are being made. Further, it fails to ask the crucial question of whether prostitution can lead to social and sexual equality for women or will in fact continue to reinforce gender disparities of rights and status. . . .

The issue of choice and consent as an analytical tool is worthless to understand prostitution as an institution. Prostitution pre-exists as a system that requires a supply of female bodies and, therefore, women and girls will be kidnapped, deceived, enticed or persuaded to ensure that supply. How women get into prostitution is irrelevant to the functioning of the prostitution system, rather, prostitution maintains itself as a system by what is and can be done to women in prostitution, and what sexual privileges prostitution allows the male clientele. . . .

Some prostitutes and prostitutes' rights advocates vigorously assert the possibility of the integrity of women's agency in prostitution and accuse anti-prostitution feminists of being patronizing and disrespectful of their perspectives.

The issue of consent, of "personal choice politics" rests on a western liberal understanding of human rights that elevates individual will and choice above all other human values and above notions of common good. At the same time, it must be noted that as a result of advances in bio-technology, the concept of personal choice has been questioned and ethical issues have been raised regarding the integrity of the human body and person, for example in connection with the sale of human organs, surrogate motherhood or human cloning. Individual choice is also generally not accepted as an argument for drug use. In defense of a conception of the human and of social good, human community has often seen the necessity to mark the boundaries of personal liberty. But perhaps because mainstream concepts of social good have never included the good of the class of women, the traditionally "socially subjugated," it is tolerated that prostitution, a "practice . . . (that) integrally contributes to the maintenance of an underclass," be accepted on the basis that some few women are freely choosing it. On that same basis, slavery might have been accepted following the few slave voices who declared that they were content with their lot.

Survivors of Prostitution and Trafficking Manifesto

We, survivors from Belgium, Denmark, Korea, the UK and the United States declare:

1. Prostitution must be eliminated. Thus, it should not be legalized or promoted.

2. Trafficked and prostituted women need services to help them create a future outside of prostitution, including legal and fiscal amnesty, financial assistance, job training, employment, housing, health services, legal advocacy, residency permits, and cultural mediators and language training for victims of international trafficking.

3. Women in prostitution need governments to punish traffickers, pimps and men who buy women for prostitution and to provide safety and security from those who would harm them.

4. Stop arresting women and arrest the perpetrators of trafficking and prostitution.

5. Stop police harassment of women in prostitution and deportation of trafficked women.

6. Prostitution is not "sex work," and sex trafficking is not "migration for sex work." Governments should stop legalizing and decriminalizing the sex industry and giving pimps and buyers legal permission to abuse women in prostitution.

As survivors of prostitution and trafficking, we will continue to strengthen and broaden our unity, help any woman out of prostitution, and work with our allies to promote the human rights of victims of trafficking and prostitution.

Survivors of Prostitution and Trafficking
Manifesto Press Conference—European Parliament,
"Who Represents Women in Prostitution?" October 17, 2005.

Right to Work

Pro-prostitution advocates invoke the right to work. However, the question begs why this work exists in the first place and why an experience of human intimacy has been transformed into the category of sexual labor. Two views are presented, either that prostitution is work like any other such as typing or waitressing, or that it fulfills a number of socially useful functions: sex education, sex therapy, or providing sex for persons who would otherwise be deprived of sex, for example, male migrant workers without their families and disabled or old men. Following this view, prostitution is said to be a rational choice of work. This view also holds that men in every circumstance and at all cost must be able to have sex.

In fact, it is the millions of buyers of sex, far outnumbering the women and girls that they use, who are not only choosing but ardently defending their practice of prostitution. But their choice is not only unexamined and unquestioned, it is brushed aside by such international agencies as the World Health Organization that in a Geneva report on AIDS in 1988 devoted pages to the socio-economic and cultural profiles of women in prostitution and in a terse paragraph stated that "Clients are more numerous than the providers of sex services. . . . The factors which lead persons to become clients are largely unknown." The general refusal to devote critical scrutiny or to assign responsibility to the users of prostitution, who constitute by far the more important component of the prostitution system is nothing less than tacit defense of male sexual privilege and practice.

The view on the right to work further holds that where there are inadequate, poor or outright bad economic options for women, prostitution may be the best option and that in any case, it is work that does no one any harm because the two parties most directly involved agree to what will happen in the prostitution exchange. This fails to acknowledge that, in fact, violence is often done to women in prostitution not just because laws do not protect women or that work conditions are not what they should be, but because men's prostitution use of women and the acts carried out are sexual enactments of a culture and system of subordination of women. Therefore, violence and degradation, even when not acted out, are inherent conditions of prostitution sex. For one thing, the possibility of violence is always present; for another, sex mediated by money means power to dictate what sex will happen. A client encountering refusal of a particular sex act or even condomless sex by a prostitute (or a wife, for that matter) will merely hire another woman who may be needier and will accept his demands. Harm will therefore be inflicted to another, more vulnerable woman.

Prostitution has been called a victimless crime, because women are assumed to consent and therefore no harm is done. The notion of harmlessness does not take into account the issue of human intimacy that is being transgressed. Women in prostitution have told of the elaborate means they employ: refusing access to some part of their bodies or the use of their own beds, creating fictional life stories or other such measures, as attempts to preserve some part of an emotional or sexual life that is theirs alone and not for public use. The view that repeated invasions of the body, of unwanted but tolerated sexual acts can be passed over harmlessly, is questionable, to say the least. Women survivors of prostitution in the Philippines like those of WHISPER (Women Hurt in Systems of Prostitution Engaged in Revolt) in the US have known "the act of prostitution as intrusive, unwanted, and often overtly violent sex that women endure." In fact, the "work" of prostitution mostly consists of submitting to acts carried out by clients or by pornographers on women's (and children's) bodies. Women repeatedly tell of strategies to finish quickly with a client, for if women need and want the money of prostitution, they do not want the sex of prostitution which as such, is a form of "paid rape."

Merely accepting the fact that there are sometimes no better work options for women is to give up the political battle for women's non-prostitution economic empowerment and to tolerate the growing operations of enormously lucrative sex businesses that absorb women as the raw material for their industry. Feminists in solidarity with women in prostitution carry out much work with and directly for them while they are in prostitution, precisely recognizing that social and economic life is designed by patriarchal capitalism to allow women few good options and that getting out of prostitution systems is a difficult process.

Sex as Biological Need

The second view of prostitution as socially useful work assumes that male need for sex is an unquestioned biological need likened to the need for food. This obviously contradicts evidence that people, women and men both, have been known to go for long periods without sex and without the fatal outcome that going without food would have! What is true is that a culture of sexual consumerism has been stoked by patriarchal capitalism and that not only is sex used to sell products of all kinds, sex itself has been reduced to an aggressively marketed product. This is a relentlessly gendered capitalist enterprise that offers the bodies of women, girls and also boys, for consumption. But it must be recognized that there are pre-existing and socially constructed sexist concepts of sexuality on which patriarchal capitalism feeds and which are not simply biologically determined. . . .

Prostitution is possible because men's power as a dominating class over women exists. The existence of some men in prostitution is in fact most often in service of other men and even when it is women who are the clients, the commercial exchange still mirrors class, race, age or other power differentials between the buyer and the bought. Most importantly, the prostitution of individual men never diminishes the power of men as a class while the prostitution of women is a direct result of and serves to maintain the subordinate status of women. It is true, of course, that class, race and other factors also operate in many other labor or employment situations. But prostitution is more than "work," it is "the most systematic institutionalized reduction of women to sex." In a 1992 UN document, the impact of prostitution on women as a class was recognized: "By reducing women to a commodity to be bought, sold, appropriated, exchanged or acquired, prostitution affected women as a group. It reinforced the societal equation of women to sex which reduced women to being less than human and contributed to sustaining women's second class status throughout the world."

Right to Freedom of Expression

The system of prostitution that includes pornography and sexual entertainment in all its forms is defended as erotic art or as sexual freedom and expression. Invoked here is the exercise of the right to freedom of expression. Strippers and other performers have sometimes even claimed to derive a sense of power in displaying sex that the male viewers are aroused to want but cannot have from the performer. In fact, it is not true that men cannot have sex when they want it; millions of women and children all over the world are trafficked into prostitution houses precisely so that men can have sex whenever and however they want, and without bounds. Sex is bought and it is inflicted: sexual crimes of rape, incest, sexual harassment are prevalent everywhere: rape occurs every 6 minutes in the United States, every 1 1/2 minute in South Africa. . . .

It is clear that sexuality was and remains political terrain where war continues to be waged against women as such practices as rape, female genital mutilation, the denial of possibilities of contraception, discrimination against lesbians, pornography or "snuff" films where sex acts culminate in the actual death of the woman make quite plain. In this war, prostitution is a main battleground where women as a class are reduced to sex, denied equal humanity, and delivered up to such practices.

To purport to promote women's sexual liberation by abstracting prostitution and pornography from male supremacist and woman-hating sexual ideology and practice is disingenuous and exposes women to harm. And while pro-prostitution advocates like to promote themselves as being "pro-sex" and to charge prostitution opponents as being "anti-sex" or "sex prudes," it is quite remarkable how they never question basic patriarchal assumptions and male sexual norms and practices. This amounts to complicity with those assumptions and practices or at the very least, to acceptance of the ideological proposition that men have a "naturally" great need for sex, including in the above forms, that must be catered to at all cost. Once again, this view willfully ignores the social and cultural construction of sexual attitudes and behavior.

To be pro-sex is to oppose prostitution by reclaiming and reconstructing a sexuality that is life-enhancing, mutually respectful and beneficial and if it is heterosexual, based on gender equality. This is by far the more revolutionary position; the pro-prostitution position is merely one of accommodation with the masculinist system already in place.

The Human Right Not to Be Prostituted

The true human rights that all women must enjoy begin with the right to non discrimination on the basis of sex that is enshrined in all major human rights instruments. Prostitution violates this right because it is a system of extreme discrimination of one group of human beings put in sexual servitude by and for the benefit of another group of human beings, and there is no denying that the overwhelming historical and majority phenomenon is of women and girls being prostituted. It violates the right to physical and moral integrity by the alienation of women's sexuality that is appropriated, debased and turned into a thing to be bought and sold. It violates the prohibition of torture and of cruel, inhuman or degrading treatment or punishment because practices of sexual "entertainment" and pornography as well as clients' acts are acts of power and violence over the female body. It violates the right to liberty and security and the prohibition of slavery, of forced labour and of trafficking in persons because millions of women and girls all over the world are held in sexual slavery to meet the demand of ever more millions of male buyers of sex and to generate profits for the capitalists of sex. It violates the right to enjoy the highest standard of physical and mental health because violence, disease, unwanted pregnancies, unsafe abortions, and AIDS stalk, presenting grave risks for women and girls in prostitution and militating against a healthy sense of and relationship with their own bodies.

Accepting or promoting prostitution as an inevitable social arrangement of sexuality or as fitting work for women denies the efforts to achieve higher standards of human rights, including the human rights of women, for example as articulated in the Beijing Platform for Action. And although even here, the lobby for the recognition of acceptable categories of prostitution has made headway through the use of the language of "forced" and "free" prostitution, the document is not consistent throughout, evidence of a continuing discomfort with that proposition. The incompatibility of prostitution with a conception of true sexual self-determination and freedom is articulated in the Platform for Action: "The human rights of women include their right to have control over and decide freely and responsibly on matters related to their sexuality, including sexual and reproductive health, free of coercion, discrimination and violence. Equal relationships between women and men in matters of sexual relations and reproduction, including full respect for the integrity of the person, require mutual respect, consent and shared responsibility for sexual behaviour and its consequences."

Prostitution must be recognized not only as part but as a foundation of the larger system of patriarchal subordination of women. Feminists have a duty to imagine a world without prostitution as we have learned to imagine a world without slavery, apartheid, infanticide or female genital mutilation. Ultimately gender relations must be restructured so that sexuality can once again be an experience of human intimacy and not a commodity to be bought or sold.

> "Governments should respect a woman's right to make decisions regarding her reproductive life."

Women Have the Right to Abortion

Center for Reproductive Rights

The Center for Reproductive Rights is a nonprofit legal advocacy organization dedicated to promoting and defending women's reproductive rights worldwide. In the following viewpoint the organization asserts that all women have the right to safe and legal abortions. The group maintains that this right is part of the basic human rights to good health, nondiscriminatory practices, and reproductive choice. It urges all governments to respect women's rights to make reproductive decisions and encourages them to support the establishment of medical facilities that will provide women with access to high-quality reproductive health-care, including abortions.

As you read, consider the following questions:

1. Each year, about how many women have unwanted pregnancies?

2. According to the World Health Organization (WHO), about how many women have unsafe abortions every year?

3. What are some long-term disabilities women may suffer from having unsafe abortions?

Each year, nearly 70 million women have unwanted pregnancies. The impact of these pregnancies will vary immensely depending on such factors as a woman's health, family relationships, economic resources, and the availability of medical care. These and other factors will influence her decision to either carry a pregnancy to term or seek an abortion. Given the complexity of this decision, the only person equipped to make it is the pregnant woman herself.

Governments should respect a woman's human right to make decisions regarding her reproductive life. A woman who decides to have an abortion—as 46 million women do annually—must have access to the facilities and care that will enable her to terminate her pregnancy safely. Governments that prosecute and punish women who have had abortions penalize women for exercising their basic rights. These rights are no less compromised when a woman who decides to terminate a pregnancy can do so only by undertaking a serious risk to her life and health. . . .

Women's Right to Life

The right to life is protected in multiple human rights instruments. It is widely acknowledged that in countries in which abortion is legally restricted, women seek abortions clandestinely, under conditions that are medically unsafe and therefore life-threatening. According to the World Health Organization (WHO), about 20 million women have unsafe abortions every year. These unsafe abortions are responsible for the deaths of nearly 70,000 women annually.

Because unsafe abortion is closely associated with high rates of maternal mortality, laws that force women to resort to unsafe procedures infringe upon women's right to life. In 2000, in interpreting Article 6.1 of the International Covenant on Civil and Political Rights, the United Nations Human Rights Committee called upon states to inform the committee of "any measures taken by the State to help women prevent unwanted pregnancies, and to ensure that they do not have to undergo life-threatening clandestine abortions."

While the phrase "right to life" has been associated with the campaigns of those who oppose abortion, it has not been interpreted in any international setting to require restrictions on abortion. Most recently [as of 2004], the European Court of Human Rights, in the case of *Vo vs. France*, stated that "it is neither desirable, nor even possible as matters stand, to answer in the abstract the question whether the unborn child is a person for the purpose of Article 2 of the Convention . . ." (providing that "[e]veryone's right to life shall be protected by law"). The court therefore refused to adopt a ruling that would have called into question the validity of laws permitting abortion in 39 member states of the Council of Europe.

Women's Right to Health

International law guarantees women the right to "the highest attainable standard of health." Unsafe abortion can have devastating effects on women's health. Where death does not result from unsafe abortion, women may experience long-term disabilities, such as uterine perforation, chronic pelvic pain or pelvic inflammatory disease.

The WHO defines "health" as "a state of complete physical, mental and social well-being, not merely the absence of disease or infirmity." While the right to health does not guarantee perfect health for all women, it has been interpreted to require governments to provide health care and to work toward creating conditions conducive to the enjoyment of good

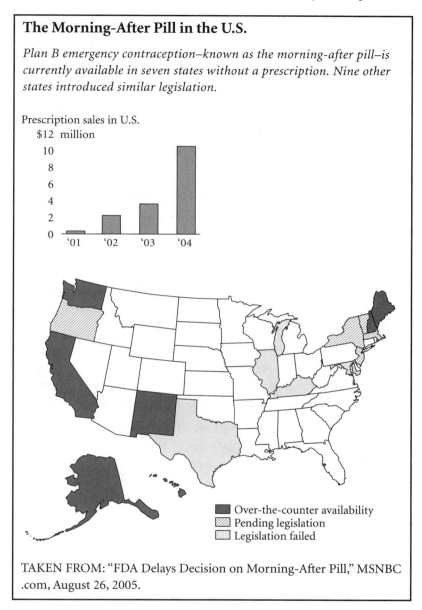

The Morning-After Pill in the U.S.

Plan B emergency contraception—known as the morning-after pill—is currently available in seven states without a prescription. Nine other states introduced similar legislation.

Prescription sales in U.S.

- Over-the-counter availability
- Pending legislation
- Legislation failed

TAKEN FROM: "FDA Delays Decision on Morning-After Pill," MSNBC .com, August 26, 2005.

health. In the context of abortion, this right to health can be interpreted to require governments to take appropriate measures to ensure that women are not exposed to the risks of unsafe abortion. Such measures include removing legal restrictions on abortion and ensuring access to high-quality abortion services.

The Programme of Action adopted at the United Nations International Conference on Population and Development (ICPD) in 1994 called upon governments to consider the consequences of unsafe abortion on women's health. It states that governments should "deal with the health impact of unsafe abortion as a major public health concern."

At the 1995 Fourth World Conference on Women, the international community reiterated this language and urged governments to "consider reviewing laws containing punitive measures against women who have undergone illegal abortions." In addition, in a paragraph addressing research on women's health, the Platform for Action urges governments "to understand and better address the determinants and consequences of unsafe abortion."

In 1999, at the five-year review of the ICPD, governments approved a provision recognizing the need for greater safety and availability of abortion services. Paragraph 63(iii) states that "[I]n circumstances where abortion is not against the law, health systems should train and equip health-service providers and should take other measures to ensure that such abortion is safe and accessible. Additional measures should be taken to safeguard women's health."

Women's Right to Nondiscrimination

The right to gender equality is a fundamental principle of human rights law. Freedom from discrimination in the enjoyment of protected human rights is ensured in every major human rights instrument.

According to the Convention on the Elimination of All Forms of Discrimination against Women, "discrimination against women" includes laws that have either the "effect" or the "purpose" of preventing a woman from exercising any of

Support for *Roe vs. Wade* Declines to Lowest Level Ever

The Harris Poll® has been measuring attitudes toward the *Roe vs. Wade* decision legalizing abortion ever since it was decided by the Supreme Court in 1973. During the 33 years since then, Harris Polls found majorities, between 52 and 65 percent of all U.S. adults, in favor of *Roe vs. Wade*. Now, a new Harris Poll finds that *Roe vs. Wade* is supported only by a slender 49 percent to 47 percent plurality. In other words, support and opposition are almost equal.

"In 1973, the U.S. Supreme Court decided that states laws which made it illegal for a woman to have an abortion up to three months of pregnancy were unconstitutional and that the decision on whether a woman should have an abortion up to three months of pregnancy should be left to the woman and her doctor to decide. In general, do you favor or oppose this part of the U.S. Supreme Court decision making abortions up to three months of pregnancy legal?"

Base: All Adults

"Support for Roe vs. Wade *Declines to Lowest Level Ever,"*
The Harris Poll, www.harrisinteractive.com/harris_poll/
index.asp?PID=659, May 4, 2006.

her human rights or fundamental freedoms on a basis of equality with men. *Laws that ban abortion have just that effect and that purpose.*

Restricting abortion has the *effect* of denying women access to a procedure that may be necessary for their enjoyment of their right to health. Only women must live with the physical and emotional consequences of unwanted pregnancy. Some women suffer maternity-related injuries, such as hemorrhage or obstructed labor. Denying women access to medical services that enable them to regulate their fertility or terminate a dangerous pregnancy amounts to a refusal to provide health care that only women need. Women are consequently exposed to health risks not experienced by men.

Laws that deny access to abortion, whatever their stated objectives, have the *discriminatory purpose* of both denigrating and undermining women's capacity to make responsible decisions about their bodies and their lives. Indeed, governments may find the potential consequences of allowing women to make such decisions threatening in some circumstances. Recognizing women's sexual and reproductive autonomy contradicts long-standing social norms that render women subordinate to men in their families and communities. It is not surprising that unwillingness to allow women to make decisions about their own bodies often coincides with the tendency to deny women decision-making roles in the areas of political, economic, social, and cultural affairs.

Women's Right to Reproductive Self-Determination

A woman has a right to make decisions regarding her own body. Support for this right is found in a number of human rights instruments, which ensure freedom in decision-making about private matters. Such provisions include protections of the right to physical integrity, the right to decide freely and responsibly the number and spacing of one's children and the right to privacy.

When a pregnancy is unwanted, its continuation can take a heavy toll on a woman's physical and emotional well-being. Decisions one makes about one's body, particularly one's reproductive capacity, lie squarely in the domain of private decision-making. Only a pregnant woman knows whether she is ready to have a child, and governments should play no role in making that decision for her.

Respect for a woman's right to plan her family requires governments to make abortion services legal, safe and accessible to all women. There are a number of circumstances in which abortion may be a woman's only means of exercising this right. A woman who becomes pregnant through an act of nonconsensual sex would be forced to bear a child were she denied her right to an abortion. For women who live in settings in which family planning services and education are unavailable, access to safe abortion services may be the only means of controlling their family size. Finally, contraceptive failure will inevitably occur among some of those women who regularly use contraception.

"It is because I still believe so strongly in the right of a woman to protect her body that I now oppose abortion."

Women Do Not Have the Right to Abortion

Frederica Mathewes-Green

Frederica Mathewes-Green is the author of seven books and many articles focusing on topics ranging from Christianity to marriage and family to popular culture. In the following viewpoint she argues that women do not have the right to have abortions because to do so would supercede the rights of their unborn children. She asserts that women suffer physically and mentally from abortions and that if an end to abortions is sought, then society must support women in the home and in the workplace so that having and caring for children becomes less taxing and more desirable.

As you read, consider the following questions:

1. The abortion industry makes about how much profit per year?
2. By what percentage did the rate of ectopic pregnancies rise between 1970 and 1987?

Frederica Mathewes-Green, "Abortion: Women's Rights ... and Wrongs," *www.femi nistsforlife.org*, 2006. Reproduced by permission.

3. About how many women who have abortions admit that they were not using contraceptives?

The abortion debate seems like an unresolvable conflict of rights: the right of women to control their own bodies, the right of children to be born. Can one both support women's rights and oppose abortion?

Times Have Changed

Truly supporting women's rights must involve telling the truth about abortion and working for it to cease. Many years ago, I felt differently; in college I advocated the repeal of abortion laws, and supported my friends who traveled for out-of-state abortions. In those early days of feminism, women faced daunting obstacles. The typical woman was thought to be charmingly silly, prone to having parking lot fender-benders and then consoling herself with a new hat. Certainly not someone who should run a corporation—perhaps someone who should not even vote.

But the hurdles were not only political: we felt physically vulnerable, as rape statistics rose and women's bodies were exploited in advertising and entertainment. The external world's disparagement of our abilities was compounded by the extra cruelty that our bodies were at risk as well from violence without and invasion within. For an unplanned pregnancy felt like an invader, an evil alien bent on colonizing one's body and destroying one's plans. The first right must be to keep one's body safe, private and healthy; without that, all other rights are meaningless.

It is because I still believe so strongly in the right of a woman to protect her body that I now oppose abortion. That right must begin when her body begins, and it must be hers no matter where she lives—even if she lives in her mother's womb. The same holds true for her brother.

119

Abortion Is Violent

For years I bought the line that the unborn was just a "glob of tissue." When I ran across a description of a mid-pregnancy abortion. I was horrified at the description of the syringe's hub jerking against the mother's abdomen as her child went through his death throes. I learned that early abortions are no more kind: the child is pulled apart limb from limb and sucked through a narrow tube to a bloody bag. Worst of all, I learned that in 1981 Dr. Willard Cates of the Centers for Disease Control estimated that 400–500 times a year children are born alive after late abortions, and then made to die—by strangulation, by drowning, or just left in a bedpan in a dark closet until the whimpering ceases.

I could not deny that this was hideous violence. Even if there were any doubt that the unborn were a person, if I had seen someone doing this to a kitten I would have been horrified. The feminism that hoped to create a new just society had embraced as essential an act of injustice. . . . Not just one death lies beneath this edifice, but tens of millions with thousands more every day. Justice cannot be built on such a bloody foundation.

Women Suffer from Abortions

Have women profited from abortion legality? Someone has profited, but not the woman who undergoes an abortion. The abortion industry makes about $500 million per year, and the sale of unborn children's parts could push that figure into the billions. The average woman does not gain, but loses, when she has an abortion. She loses first the hundreds of dollars cash she must pay to receive the surgery. Second, she must undergo a humiliating procedure, an invasion deeper than rape, as the interior of her uterus is crudely vacuumed to remove every scrap of life. Some women will be haunted by the sound of that vacuum the rest of their lives.

Third, she can lose her health. A woman's body is a delicately balanced ecology, not meant to have its natural, healthy process disrupted by invasive machinery. In addition to the women who are punctured or killed on abortion tables, there are more subtly damaging effects. The opening of the uterus, the cervix, is designed to open gradually over several days at the end of a pregnancy. In an abortion, the cervix is wrenched open in a matter of minutes. The delicate muscle fibers can be damaged—damage that may go unnoticed until she is far into a later, wanted pregnancy and the muscles give way in a miscarriage.

While the cervix can be opened, the uterus was never intended to be vacuumed. Nicks and scratches can cause scarring which may lead to endometriosis. But if those scars are near the fallopian tubes, the openings can be partly obliterated. Tiny sperm can swim in and fertilize the egg, but the fertilized egg, hundreds of times larger than a sperm, cannot pass back through into the uterus. The fertilized egg can implant and grow in a tube until the child's size reaches the tube's limit; if the condition is not diagnosed the tube explodes, the child dies and the mother may die. When I read that the rate of ectopic pregnancy in America rose 500% between 1970 and 1987, it's almost too obvious to ask what was the single greatest change in women's reproductive health care during that time. But of course the multiplication of ectopic-related injuries is taken as proof that pregnancy is more dangerous than abortion.

Alternatively, the scarring at the tube's entrance may be complete. In this case the sperm can never meet the egg, and the woman is sterile; she thought she was aborting one pregnancy, but she was aborting all her pregnancies for the rest of her life.

Loss of Peace of Mind

Which brings us to the most devastating loss of all; she loses her own child. Abortion rhetoric paints the unborn as a para-

Parental Consent or Notification for Abortion

- ☐ States requiring parental consent
- States requiring parental notification
- States requiring knowledge and/or notification and consent
- States with no abortion laws specific to minors

TAKEN FROM: The National Conference of State Legislatures, "Parental Consent or Notification for Abortion," www.ncsl .org, January 2004.

site, a lump, that "glob of tissue." But it is in fact her own child as much like her as any child she will ever have, sharing her appearance, talents, and family tree. In abortion, she offers her own child as a sacrifice for the right to continue her life, and it is a sacrifice that will haunt her.

For the last loss is the loss of her peace of mind. Many women grieve silently after abortion, their sorrow ignored by a society that expects them to be grateful for the "freedom" to abort. Some suffer depression, nightmares, suicidal thoughts; some wake in the night thinking they hear a baby crying. A man who saw his wife slowly disintegrate after her abortion asks, "What kind of trade-off is that, gain control of your body, lose control of your mind?" The baby lost in an abortion is not one that will keep her mom awake at night—at least not right away.

For all these losses, women gain nothing but the right to run in place. Abortion doesn't cure any illness, it doesn't win any woman a raise. But in a culture that treats pregnancy and childbearing as impediments, it surgically adapts the woman to fit in. If women are an oppressed group they are the only such group to require surgery in order to be equal. In Greek mythology, Procrustes was an exacting host if you were the wrong size for his bed, he would stretch or chop you to fit. The abortion table is modern feminism's Procrustean bed, one that, in a hideous twist, its victims actually march in the streets to demand.

Earlier strains of feminism saw this issue more clearly. Susan B. Anthony called abortion "child murder" and called for "prevention, not merely punishment . . . [of] the dreadful deed." The nineteenth-century feminists were unanimous in opposing abortion. Elizabeth Cady Stanton grouped it with infanticide and proclaimed that if it was degrading to treat women as property, it was no better for women to treat their own children as property. Perhaps their colleague Mattie Brinkerhoff was clearest when she likened a woman seeking abortion to a man who steals because he is hungry.

Women Are Desperate

For the question remains, do women want abortion? Not like she wants a Porsche or an ice cream cone. Like an animal caught in a trap, trying to gnaw off its own leg, a woman who seeks an abortion is trying to escape a desperate situation by an act of violence and self-loss. Abortion is not a sign that women are free, but a sign that they are desperate.

How did such desperation become so prevalent? Two trends in modern feminism, both adapted from the values of the masculine power structure that preceded it, combine to necessitate abortion. Re-emerging feminism was concerned chiefly with opening doors for women to professional and public life, and later embraced advocacy of sexual freedom as well. Yet participation in public life is significantly complicated by responsibility for children, while uncommitted sexual activity is the most effective way of producing unwanted pregnancies. This dilemma—simultaneous pursuit of behaviors that cause children and that are hampered by children—inevitably finds its resolution on an abortion table.

If we were to imagine a society that instead supports and respects women, we would have to begin with preventing these unplanned pregnancies. Contraceptives fail, and half of all aborting women admit they weren't using them anyway. Thus, preventing unplanned pregnancies will involve a return to sexual responsibility. This means either avoiding sex in situations where a child cannot be welcomed, or being willing to be responsible for lives unintentionally conceived, perhaps by making an adoption plan, entering a marriage, or faithful child support payments. Using contraceptives is no substitute for this responsibility, any more than wearing a safety belt gives one the right to speed. The child is conceived through no fault of her own; it is the height of cruelty to demand the right to shred her in order to continue having sex without commitment.

Help Women Care for Children

Second, we need to make continuing a pregnancy and raising a child less of a burden. Most agree that women should play a part in the public life of our society, their talents and abilities are as valuable as men's, and there is no reason to restrict them from the employment sphere. But during the years that her children are young, mother and child usually prefer to be together. If women are to be free to take off these years in the middle of a career, they must have, as above, faithful, responsible men who will support them. Both parents can also benefit from more flexibility in the workplace: allowing parents of school-age children to set their hours to coincide with the school day, for example, or enabling more workers to escape the expenses of office, commute, and childcare by working from home. We must also welcome women back into the workforce when they want to return, accounting their years at home as valuable training in management, education, and negotiating skills.

Women's rights are not in conflict with their own children's rights; the appearance of such a conflict is a sign that something is wrong in society. When women have the sexual respect and employment flexibility they need, they will no longer seek as a substitute the bloody injustice of abortion.

Periodical Bibliography

The following articles have been selected to supplement the diverse views presented in this chapter.

Susan J. Brison — "Contentious Freedom: Sex Work and Social Construction," *Hypatia*, Fall 2006.

Ebony — "Back to Basics," March 2007.

Julie Hanus — "We Don't Need Another Wave: Dispatches from the Next Generation of Feminists," *Utne*, November–December 2006.

Michelle Humphrey — "Bare Necessity on Porn and Progress," *Bitch Magazine: Feminist Response to Pop Culture*, Summer 2006.

Maggie Mortimer — "How to Stop Female Genital Mutilation," *Herizons*, Winter 2007.

New Statesman — "The Fallacy of the 'Easy Girl' Generation," August 14, 2006.

Emily Nussbaum — "The Feminine Mistake," *New York*, November 13, 2006.

Angela Phillips — "The Rise and Fall of 'Silent Girly-Gifts in G-strings,'" *Times Higher Education Supplement*, July 14, 2006.

Frances Cohen Praver — "Daring Wives: Why Women Cheat," *USA Today Magazine*, March 2007.

Stephanie Rosenbloom — "A Disconnect on Hooking Up," *New York Times*, March 1, 2007.

Stacy Schiff — "Desperately Seeking Susan," *New York Times*, October 13, 2007.

Peng Yen-Wen — "Buying Sex," *Men & Masculinities*, January 2007.

OPPOSING
VIEWPOINTS®
SERIES

CHAPTER 3

How Has Feminism Affected Women's Roles in the Workplace?

Chapter Preface

A study released in February 2007 by researchers at Harvard and McGill universities reveals startling facts about the conditions of working parents in the United States. According to their data, the United States is one of only five countries in the world that does not guarantee any form of paid maternity leave, making it the only wealthy nation that does not provide this benefit. Furthermore, the United States is among only a handful of countries that does not mandate statutory paid sick leave or other types of paid annual leave. Regrettably, the lack of such benefits has made going to work challenging for parents, especially for mothers who still bear the brunt of most childcare responsibilities.

Although the situation for working parents improved in 1993 with the passage of the Family and Medical Leave Act (FMLA), the benefits remain limited. While the FMLA entitles most workers up to 12 weeks of job-protected medical leave for birth or adoption, it does not cover employees who work for smaller companies and guarantees only unpaid leaves. Therefore, new parents must pull together remaining sick days, vacation days, and even short-term disability to ensure that they are paid at least a partial salary while they stay home with their children. Although there are some notable exceptions, most companies do not offer more parental leave options than the law requires.

Jody Heymann, Alison Earle, and Jeffrey Hayes, the authors of the study discussed above, offer many reasons why parental benefits are important. They argue that such benefits will improve children's health outcomes by allowing parents time to focus on the well-being of the entire family. Having paid leave time will also improve the economic conditions of families with children because parents will not have to quit their jobs or risk losing them to care for their children. Most importantly, for companies concerned about the effects of such politics on their bottom line, providing parental leave benefits will reduce employee turnover, which can reduce recruitment and training costs. According to an article by Jodie Levin-Epstein in the *American Prospect*, businesses, like IKEA, that offer paid family leave benefit in multiple ways, such as fewer employee absences and lower health care costs. Her research revealed that "highly stressed workers create health expenditures nearly 50 percent greater than those with low stress."

As is revealed by some of the viewpoints in this chapter, not all feminists believe that workplace conditions for working parents are as dire as some may argue. In fact, many feminists argue that by choosing to have children, women are necessarily choosing to make less money and risking future workplace advancement. In addition, many companies have argued that providing paid family leave benefits is too costly. In fact, a recent bill that would mandate paid parental leave in Colorado was withdrawn by its author, Terrance Carroll, after he spoke to corporate leaders in the state who felt that it would put "an undue burden on business." Although the future of parental leave policies remains unclear, as women continue to enter the workforce and move up the corporate ladder in greater numbers, work-life balance issues will remain at the forefront of debate.

> *"In short, it is women's life and career choices—not a patriarchal society—that result in women earning less than men."*

Women Choose to Make Less Than Men

Arrah Nielsen

Arrah Nielsen is a freelance writer and a former junior fellow at Independent Women's Forum on whose Web site the following viewpoint appears. She argues that the wage gap between women and men is a myth. It only appears that women make less money than men because the jobs that women choose to do pay less and require less hours than those occupations chosen by men. Also, Nielsen asserts that women take far longer breaks from the workplace than men so that they can care for their children and households. She urges young women to make better choices in their own careers.

As you read, consider the following questions:

1. How many more times are women more likely than men to take time out of the workforce?

Arrah Nielsen, "Working Girl," *www.iwf.org*, July 15, 2005. Reproduced with permission by Independent Women's Forum. www.iwf.org.

2. According to surveys, what percentage of female MBA graduates do not work outside the home ten years after graduation?

3. According to a study by Kern and Ferry, what percentage of women say they want to be CEOs of companies as compared to men?

Feminist groups have parroted the statistic that women earn only 76 cents to the male dollar so many times that it is seldom challenged by the mainstream media or anywhere else in the popular culture. Feminist groups imply that the wage gap is due to discrimination and that all women are victims.

But college women getting ready to graduate and find a job should take heart. The wage gap is a misleading statistic that fails to account for several crucial factors impacting women's wages such as:

- Time worked. Women take much more time out of the workforce and assume a greater share of the domestic load. Long, uninterrupted employment correlates with higher wages.

- College majors and career choices. Women disproportionately major in the social sciences and enter lower paying, but more personally fulfilling, careers such as elementary education and social work. Bachelor's degrees in the hard sciences and technology command higher incomes than those in the liberal arts.

- Playing it safe. Women are generally less willing than men to take dangerous or unpleasant jobs that offer higher wages to offset the extra risk.

In short, it is women's life and career choices—not a patriarchal conspiracy—that result in women earning less than men. The best way to boost women's earnings is to inform them of why men earn more and leave the choices and the consequences up to them. . . .

What Is the Wage Gap?

Equal pay for equal work has been enforced by the Equal Employment Opportunity Act since it was made law in 1972. The Equal Pay Act of 1963 and Title VII of the Civil Rights Act of 1964 also banned sex-based wage discrimination. So it seems pretty remarkable that the wage gap is so wide and pervasive today. Attorneys should be having a field day with class action lawsuits over this grave injustice. But they are not. Could it be that even the legal establishment is itself involved in this glaringly obvious patriarchal conspiracy?

Fortunately, no. The wage gap is a misleading statistic. It compares all women to all men. Thus, the male orthopedic surgeon working in excess of 70 hours per week is tossed in alongside the female receptionist working 40 hour weeks. The statistic does not take into account the level of education, the years of work, and the choice of education. And these factors can have a big impact on how much money you make.

For example, the Bureau of Labor Statistics reports "that the average person working 45 hours per week earns 44 percent more pay—that is, 44 percent more pay for 13 percent more work." In other words, a small difference in number of hours worked can add up to a big difference in dollars earned. Women are 50 times more likely than men to take time out of the workforce, for care-giving and other reasons. This difference should not be overlooked when trying to get at the roots of the wage gap.

When males and females in the same occupation, with similar qualifications and experience, are compared there is virtually no difference in their pay. A definitive study of the gender wage gap conducted by economist June O'Neill, former director of the Congressional Budget Office, found that

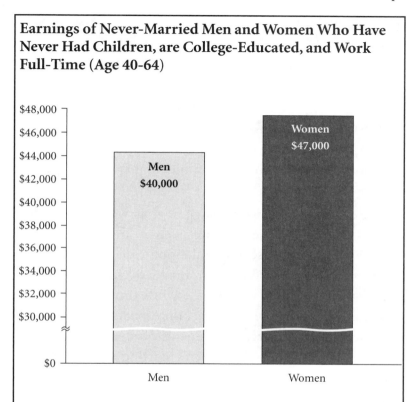

Earnings of Never-Married Men and Women Who Have Never Had Children, are College-Educated, and Work Full-Time (Age 40-64)

TAKEN FROM: Warren Ferrell, *Why Women Earn More: The Startling Truth Behind the Pay Gap—and What Women Can Do About It.* New York: AMACOM, 2005.

women earn 98 percent of what men do when controlled for experience, education, and number of years on the job.

The Choices Women Make

Warren Farrell, three time board of directors member of the National Organization for Women (NOW) New York City, points out in *Why Men Earn More* that one reason men earn more than women is they are far more likely to take unpleasant and dangerous jobs, what Farrell calls the "death and exposure professions." For example, firefighting, truck driving, mining, and logging are just a few high risk jobs that are over

95 percent male. Conversely, low risk jobs, like secretarial work or childcare, are over 95 percent female. . . .

Because men are more likely to take jobs that are unpleasant, dangerous, or dull in exchange for higher pay, they reap the financial benefit. Farrell summarizes this phenomenon this way: "jobs . . . that expose you to the sleet and the heat pay more than those that are indoors and neat." Individual women could choose to enter more risky but higher paying professions, but most choose not to.

There is little evidence to suggest that women earn less than men merely because they are women. In fact, according to the 1960 U.S. Census of Population, a decade before the Equal Pay Act was passed, never married childless college-educated white women who worked full time were earning 106 percent of what their male counterparts were making. Furthermore, Warren Farrell documents occupations requiring bachelor's degrees in which women's starting salaries actually exceed men's. Female investment bankers and dieticians, for example, can expect to earn 116 percent to 130 percent of their male counterparts' salaries.

Why then do women earn less than men? The primary reason is that on average maximizing earnings is less of a priority for women than it is for men. Men are 50 times more likely than women to be the primary or sole breadwinners for their families, and even well-educated women, who are presumably more ambitious than the average Jane, are less committed to their careers and less willing to make sacrifices for them. Surveys of female MBAs reveal that ten years after graduation, 20 percent do not work at all, having opted out of the workforce in favor of being stay-at-home moms. A Korn/Ferry study revealed that only 14 percent of women, compared to 46 percent of men, say they actually want to be a CEO.

Comparable Worth

But feminist organizations like the National Organization for Women and the Ms. Foundation don't accept these differences in decisions as the real reason for differences in pay. They argue that female-dominated occupations are undervalued. Thus they insist that women who enter occupations such as elementary education and secretarial work, which have low starting pay and little opportunity for advancement, are victims of an economic system that undervalues and undercompensates their work. They argue for "comparable worth" legislation that would have the government decide how much professions ought to be paid in order that secretaries make the same wage as truck drivers.

To proponents of comparable worth, the mere fact that female-dominated occupations such as secretarial work and childcare pay less than male-dominated jobs like construction work, which require less education, is concrete proof that women are being unfairly discriminated against. What feminists and other comparable worth proponents overlook is that it is the market, not anonymous committees of wage makers, that determines what employees are paid. Comparable worth? Comparable to what? . . .

In a free market, wages are a compromise between what employees are willing to work for and what their employers are willing to pay them. Instituting comparable worth will ultimately only hurt women and the economy by making women more expensive to employ, under-compensating certain professions causing labor surpluses and shortages, and stifling economic growth. There is simply no way that unelected bureaucrats can synthesize the full volume of information reflected in wage rates. The most accurate labor statistics available run a year behind. . . . Wages are most accurately and fairly determined by the free association of labor participants.

Hearth and Home

Another reason women's average earnings are less than men's is that they tend to shoulder a greater share of the domestic load at home, and take more time out of the workforce for care-giving. Women more than men adjust their work schedules to accommodate their families. And in poll after poll, they express a preference to do so.

"Well, why can't men and women share domestic responsibilities 50-50 so women will be just as free and unencumbered as men are?" the conventional feminist argument goes. Some couples manage to create such an arrangement, but in general couples typically find it easier for each partner to specialize and make the sacrifices required to sustain the family. Most couples find that one career has to give when children come along and it is usually the mother's.

Scholars can debate whether it is societal pressure or innate desire that makes women elect to spend more time with their children. But so long as these decisions are a reflection of women's expressed preferences, this isn't a problem that needs to be solved. . . .

Feminists have ignored how women's lives and goals differ from men's. In doing so they have overlooked the fact that women's life choices not sex discrimination—are responsible for the infamous wage gap. In order for women to reach absolute parity with men, they will have to work full time all the time, and choose career paths that pay more, but are less flexible and fulfilling. This recipe for equality is at odds with what most women want, but that does not seem to matter to feminists pushing the notion that women are shortchanged economically. They have mistaken equal opportunity for equal outcomes.

Understanding the reasons why men earn more than women, not promoting the paranoid, tiresome notion that women are victims, is the key to boosting earnings. It is the knowledge of how individual choices impact workplace earnings—not divisive ideology—that will empower women. College women should take note: the truth will set you free.

> "A large part of the wage gap is discrimi-
> natory, and only a part is due to differ-
> ences in male and female occupations."

Women Do Not Choose
to Make Less Than Men

Stephanie Seguino

*In the following viewpoint, Stephanie Seguino, professor of eco-
nomics at the University of Vermont, argues that the wage gap
between men and women still exists. Although some theorists
have posited that women's earnings remain lower than men's because of choices that they make in the workplace, Seguino de-
bunks these notions and points to gender discrimination as the
source for the inequality. Citing recent gender discrimination
cases involving Wal-Mart and Home Depot, Seguino declares
that as long as this gap persists, women, society, and especially
children will lose out on opportunities for growth and success.*

As you read, consider the following questions:

1. About how much, on the dollar, do women earn less
   than men?

2. Around what percentage of Wal-Mart's store managers
   are women as compared to men?

Stephanie Seguino, "The Wage Gap Debate Continues," *Vermont Cynic*, November 29,
2005. Copyright © 2007 *Vermont Cynic*. Reproduced by permission.

3. Around what percentage of Home Depot's newly hired women were given sales jobs as compared to newly hired men?

The Wage Gap does exist.

The problem of pay inequality between the sexes persists. Full time women workers average $30,724 in annual earnings compared to men's $40,668, or about 75.5 cents on the male dollar. Not all women and men work full time. Among all working-age adults, the gap is considerably wider—women's income is less than half men's.

The cumulative effect of the gender wage gap may surprise you. One study shows that a woman in her late 20s who works full time would lose about half a million dollars in income by the time she was in her mid 40s, compared to a similarly qualified man.

Choice or Discrimination

How you feel about the pay gap between women and men depends on whether you see it as the result of women's choices or of discrimination.

One view is that women choose to enter "female" occupations that are lower paid and require less skill and time commitment in order to care for children. Since gender inequality is the result of "choice," why worry about pay inequality?

Others say the wide sex gap in pay is due to policies and social institutions—labor markets, family, religion—which confine women to jobs characterized by low wages, little mobility, and limited prestige. Added to this, employers and male employees are seen as actively discriminating against women, who are denied promotion and training opportunities that men have.

What does the evidence tell us about the merits of these two positions? It tells us unambiguously that a large part of the wage gap is discriminatory, and only a part is due to differences in male and female occupations and women's greater time off to care for children and the elderly.

Sex Segregation of Jobs

How this happens is quite complex. Sometimes employers pay lower wages to women than men in the same workplace, but usually the process is subtler. A common phenomenon is that women and men are segregated in different jobs, making wage discrimination less obvious.

Sex segregation of jobs is a dominant feature of our economy. This is easily observed. The next time you go for a dental visit, check out the gender of the office: dental hygienists and staff tend to be female, and dentists male. Pilots, clergy, engineers, firefighters are almost entirely male. Bank tellers, childcare workers, nurses, elementary teachers are mostly female.

Less noticeable is that even if jobs don't seem segregated, most top jobs are given to men. Some people find this hard to believe.

They think these times are behind us. But two recent legal cases, involving Wal-Mart and Home Depot, remind us that employers actively work to maintain gender hierarchies in the workplace.

A class action suit was recently [as of 2005] brought against Wal-Mart, the nation's largest employer, covering 1.6 million current and former female Wal-Mart employees.

Statistical analysis shows that Wal-Mart pays female workers less and gives them fewer promotions than men. Although women make up more than 70% of Wal-Mart's hourly workforce, they are less than one-third of its store management. Even in the same job category, pay gaps exist at Wal-Mart, and the salary gap widens over time even for men and women hired into the same jobs at the same time.

At Home Depot, the story is similar. New hires are assigned either to sales jobs or to jobs as cashiers. Those in sales jobs have opportunities to move into positions as department supervisors and assistant store managers, while promotion is unlikely for cashiers. The legal case against Home Depot provided evidence that about 77% of newly hired men were given sales jobs, but only 20 percent of women.

Women were kept out of entry-level jobs that could lead to promotion. Take the case of Patty Nichols, hired as a cashier in a Houston Home Dept in 1988. She began to make inquiries about an assistant manager job after 8 years with Home Depot, a bachelor's degree in management, and a good work record. She was interviewed for the job 4 times in the next 2 years but was passed over each time for a less experienced and less knowledgeable man.

She had been given good management reviews until she filed a complaint about her treatment to the [Equal Employment Opportunity Commission] EEOC. Then her performance evaluations turned sour.

Perpetuating Gender Norms

This short story tells us about the barriers many women face in moving up the job ladder, and the reprisals they face if they challenge the gender hierarchy that keeps them at the bottom. Many women ultimately accept the status quo, but one cannot call that "choice"—acquiescence would be a better description.

These two cases indicate that at least part of the earnings gap between men and women is due to discrimination—the perpetuation of gender norms that suggest women belong at the bottom of the hierarchy.

But can employer discrimination persist in competitive markets? After all, firms that discriminate pay for it in higher labor costs.

Women Earn a Majority of Their Families' Incomes

What proportion of your family's income do you personally earn—all or almost all, more than half, about half, less than half, or none or almost none?

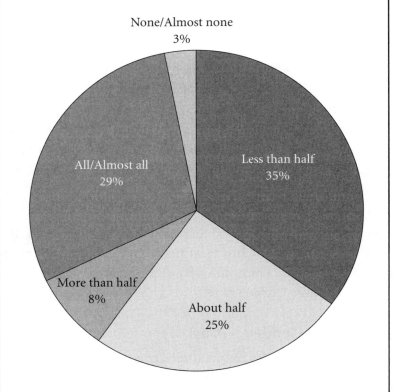

None/Almost none 3%

Less than half 35%

All/Almost all 29%

More than half 8%

About half 25%

TAKEN FROM: "Ask a Working Woman Survey Report," AFL-CIO, www.twu.org, 2004.

At least in theory, pay inequality should eventually disappear because the discriminating firms will be competed out of business. This might be true if markets were competitive, but they are not.

Certainly, Wal-Mart and Home Depot cannot be considered your run-of-the-mill small businesses that compete with local businesses on equal footing. Large companies can afford to discriminate especially if they find that putting women in supervisory positions causes men to become disruptive on the job, lowering productivity. The evidence that pay gaps persist undermines the competition argument.

Flex Time and Children

Some believe women's wages are lower because they prefer jobs that give them a flexible work schedule to be home with the kids part of the time.

But UVM's Professor Elaine McCrate finds no evidence for this explanation. She recently published a study that finds that it is men, mainly white men in upper echelon positions, whose jobs are the most flexible and the most highly paid.

Wage gaps are the result of gender hierarchies that play out at various levels of society, and are so embedded, we are often blind to the processes that lead to this inequality.

Blaming women's childcare responsibilities for their low wages suggests women are "victims of choice." But the fact is women often take care of the kids because men frequently don't. That may be a rational choice for some families. Women's lower wages make it less costly for the individual family to forgo the income of the adult with the lowest wages.

We are lucky women are willing to do this unpaid work. Society would be much worse off if our children were not well cared for.

But it is a mistake to believe that this is an optimal outcome. Our society has failed to develop policies so that women can attain economic equality and independence.

Gender pay gaps are a problem—they are a problem for fairness in a society that considers itself a meritocracy. They are a problem for the many women whose life choices are limited and who find it difficult to exit painful relationships because of inadequate income.

They are a problem in lost efficiency, because many qualified women fail to get jobs they deserve that instead go to unqualified men.

And gender pay inequality is a problem for children.

The stark fact is that gender relations are undergoing a tumultuous change, and stable relationships are no longer the norm. Many single-headed households have women at the helm. Discriminatory pay gaps leave women in precarious financial straits and contribute to children's poverty.

Rather than try to justify inequality, we would be better served by taking measures to rectify the problem.

| *"The glass-ceiling phenomenon is proving peculiarly persistent."*

The Glass Ceiling Still Exists

Economist

In the following viewpoint a staff writer at the Economist, *a weekly publication that focuses on issues in business and industry, argues that despite the presence of women in many areas of corporate culture, they remain absent in top positions. Although it is becoming more known that diversity in upper ranks can be very beneficial to most companies, women are still not appointed to or made to feel welcome in the boardroom. The writer asserts that change is necessary not only for the career advancement of women but for the future success of businesses in the global economy.*

As you read, consider the following questions:

1. In 2005, women accounted for what percentage of the U.S. workforce and what percentage of its top managers?

2. According to the results of a 2002 survey, how many women said that they aspired to be CEO as opposed to men?

3. What strategy is Norway employing to increase the number of female executives in top positions?

It is 20 years since [in 1985] the term "glass ceiling" was coined by the *Wall Street Journal* to describe the apparent barriers that prevent women from reaching the top of the corporate hierarchy, and it is ten years since the American government's specially appointed Glass Ceiling Commission published its recommendations. In 1995 the commission said that the barrier was continuing "to deny untold numbers of qualified people the opportunity to compete for and hold executive level positions in the private sector." It found that women had 45.7% of America's jobs and more than half of the master's degrees being awarded. Yet 95% of senior managers were men, and female managers' earnings were on average a mere 68% of their male counterparts'.

Ten years on, women account for 46.5% of America's workforce and for less than 8% of its top managers, although at big *Fortune* 500 companies the figure is a bit higher. Female managers' earnings now average 72% of their male colleagues'. Booz Allen Hamilton, a consulting firm that monitors departing chief executives in America, found that 0.7% of them were women in 1998, and 0.7% of them were women in 2004. In between, the figure fluctuated. But the firm says that one thing is clear: the number is "very low and not getting higher." . . .

The glass-ceiling phenomenon is proving peculiarly persistent. The top of the corporate ladder remains stubbornly male, and the few women who reach it are paid significantly less than the men that they join there.

This is despite the fact that companies are trying harder than ever to help women to climb higher. So-called "diversity programmes" (which are aimed at promoting minorities as well as women) are as common as diversity on the board is rare, and not just among service industries such as finance and retailing. No-nonsense formerly male clubs such as IBM (where two decades ago blue-suited identical white men drove the company close to bankruptcy), GE (where the culture was not exactly female-friendly during the long rule of its legendary leader Jack Welch) and BP (where long hours at sea on windy oil rigs were a career booster) have appointed senior executives to be in charge of diversity. The three firms were the unlikely joint sponsors of a recent conference on "Women in Leadership."

Diversity Pays

Such companies no longer see the promotion of women solely as a moral issue or equal opportunity and equal pay. They have been persuaded of the business case for diversity. It has long been known that mixed groups are better at problem solving than like-minded ones. But the benefits of diversity are greater than this. Research by Catalyst, an American organisation that aims to expand "opportunities for women and business," found a strong correlation between the number of women in top executive positions and financial performance among *Fortune* 500 companies between 1996 and 2000.

For some companies the push towards greater diversity has come from their customers. Lou Gerstner, the man who turned around IBM partly by promoting diversity within the company, has said "we made diversity a market-based issue . . . it's about understanding our markets, which are diverse and multicultural." Lisa Bondesio, head of diversity in Britain for Deloitte, a big firm of accountants, says that diversity is "about how we differentiate ourselves in the marketplace."

Other companies surprisingly fail to reflect the diversity of their customers. Procter & Gamble (P&G), for example, the manufacturer of Pampers nappies [diapers], Max Factor and Tampax, boasts in its 2004 annual report that it was ranked "among the top companies for executive women" by the National Association for Female Executives. Yet it has only two women on its 16-person board, both of them non-executives, and out of the 45 people it lists as its top "corporate officers" only three are women—ie, 93% of them are men. P&G is an enormously successful company and its management programmes are widely admired. Its shareholders may wonder if it would do even better if the gender ratios at the top were less skewed.

Many companies have been motivated by a desire to broaden the pool of "talent" that their human resources departments can fish in. They worry in general about the ageing populations of the developed world. But particular industries have other reasons for broadening their recruitment trawl. The big accounting firms, for example, had their reputations seriously dented by the demise of Enron and its auditor Arthur Andersen just before they had an unprecedented increase in business as a consequence of the extra duties imposed by the Sarbanes-Oxley Act. They became the "employer of choice" for far fewer graduates at a time when they needed to attract far more. A consequence is that they have had to extend their recruitment and promotion efforts to more women.

The management-consulting business, where firms tend to follow the career strategy of "up or out," would like to hold on to many more of its women. But up or out can scarcely accommodate maternity leave, so it is no surprise that the industry loses twice as many women as men from the middle rungs of its career ladder.

Booz Allen Hamilton, a leading consulting firm, regularly wonders how to alter the fact that only 1-2% of its partners are women. Orit Gadiesh, the chairman of Bain, a rival, is a notable exception to the general exclusion of women from the top ranks. However, an earlier career in the Israeli army may have provided essential skills for her to reach the top.

Successful Diversity Programs

Some firms' diversity programmes are working. At IBM, there are now seven women among its 40 top executives. GE says that 14% of its "senior executives" are now women, although none of them was featured in the chief executive's recent reshuffle at the very top. The firm's six new business divisions are all headed by men.

By contrast, Alcan, a Canadian multinational metal manufacturer, has made extraordinary progress. Three out of its four main businesses are now headed by women (including the bauxite and alumina business). Steven Price, the company's HR director, says "it's been a long journey" to reach this point. Crucial has been "the tone at the top" and a determination to break down the perception that working long hours and wearing air miles like a "battle medal" are ways to get ahead in the company.

Why is it proving so difficult for women to reach the top of corporations? Are they simply less ambitious, less excited by the idea of limitless (albeit first-class) travel, late nights and the onerous responsibilities imposed by mounting regulation? A 2002 survey of top executives in American multinationals around the world did find them to be less ambitious, at least for the very top job: 19% of the men interviewed aspired to be CEO, whereas only 9% of the women did. At a slightly lower level there was less difference: 43% of women hoped to join a senior management committee, compared with 54% of the men. Catalyst, on the other hand, says that its research shows that women and men have equal desires to have the CEO job. "Ambition knows no gender," says Ilene Lang, the president of Catalyst and once a senior executive in Silicon Valley.

Who's in the Club?

Top businesswomen in America give three main explanations for why so few of them reach "C-level"—that group of executives who preface their titles with the word "chief." First comes the exclusion from informal networks. In many firms jock-talk and late-night boozing still oil the wheels of progress. In

America and elsewhere it has become almost traditional for sales teams to take potential clients to strip clubs and the like. These activities specifically exclude most women.

Yasmin Jetha, a Muslim of Asian origin who made it to the board of Abbey, a British bank and a FTSE100 company until it was taken over last year by Spain's Banco Santander, says that although she neither drinks alcohol nor supports a rugby team, she made a point in her career of participating in industry-wide events where the opportunities for exclusion are less. More and more women in business are forming their own networks, which also help to counter male clubbishness.

The second hurdle is what Ms. Lang calls "pervasive stereotyping of women's capacity for leadership." Everyone is unconsciously biased and there is strong evidence that men are biased against promoting women inside companies. This was a central point in the landmark 1989 case in America of *Price Waterhouse vs. Hopkins*, where Ann Hopkins sued her employer when she was not given a partnership. She eventually won her case in the Supreme Court. Since then some companies have begun to take special steps to guard against bias. Deloitte, for example, carefully scrutinises its pay and promotion decisions for bias, especially its list of new partners announced annually in June.

The third hurdle is the lack of role models. There are too few women in top jobs to show how it is done. Helen Alexander, the chief executive of The Economist Group and one of very few female CEOs to have succeeded a female CEO (Ms. Scardino) says, however, that the role models that matter come earlier in life—at school or in the family. In addition, it seems to be important for many successful businesswomen to have had a supportive father.

Taking Time Off

Chris Bones, a senior human-resources executive with Cadbury Schweppes before he took over as head of Henley Man-

Women Executives

- 11.2% of corporate officers are women.

- 75% of *Fortune* 500 companies (376) have at least 1 woman officer.

- Over half (258) of *Fortune* 500 companies have more than 1 female corporate officer.

- 6% of corporate officers holding line jobs are women, while 94% are men.

- Savings institutions are the industry with the most women at the top—32% of corporate officers are women. Other top industries include: diversified financials (30%), publishing/printing (26%), and transportation equipment (24%).

- 2 industry groups have no women corporate officers: trucking and textiles; others with low representation include electronics, semiconductors (2%), and waste management (3%).

- Women make up 2.7% of top earners—the 5 most highly paid officers at *Fortune* 500 companies, compared to men who make up 97.3% of top earners.

- In November 2002, women represent 15.7% of the corporate officers in America's 500 largest companies. These percentages are up from 12.5% in 2000 and 8.7% in 1995.

- In April 2002, there were six female CEOs in the *Fortune* 500 and a total of eleven in the *Fortune* 1000.

BreaktheGlassCeiling.com, *2003–2004.*

agement College at the beginning of this year [2005], suggests another reason. The flattening of organisations in recent years, as layers of management have been stripped out, has meant that promotions now are far steeper steps than they used to be. This leaves fewer opportunities for people to re-enter the workforce at higher levels. And many women inevitably need to take time off during their careers. In America, there is evidence to suggest that more women with children under the age of one are taking time off work than was the case some years ago.

More and more too are withdrawing to care for elderly parents at a time when they are on the cusp of the higher echelons. Ben Rosen, a professor at the Kenan-Flagler Business School in North Carolina who has done research on the topic, says that many women bail out of corporate life to become self-employed consultants and entrepreneurs, roles where they can have greater freedom and autonomy to manage the rest of their lives. This may be reinforcing companies' long-held belief that they should invest less in women's careers because they are unlikely to stay the course.

Ms. Maier's Gallic analysis of the issue is that French men spend more time at work than women, which "can be explained by their insatiable predatory instincts as well as by their casual approach to banal household chores." This leaves women with so much to do at home that they are more than twice as likely as men to work part-time, "which makes it all the more impossible to break the glass ceiling." In America a survey by the Centre for Work-Life Policy found that 40% of highly qualified women with spouses felt that their husbands did less work around the home than they created.

Another finding of the study was that qualified women leave work for a mixture of reasons—some pull them away (home and family life), and some push them away (the type of work, the people they are working with). In business, the push factors were found to be particularly powerful, "unlike, say, in medicine or teaching." The vast majority of women (93%) said they wanted to return to work, but found the options available to them "few and far between, and extremely costly." Across sectors, women lost 37% of their earning power when they spent three or more years out of the workforce.

Very few (5%) wanted to return to the companies they had left, claiming the work they had been doing there was not particularly satisfying. In Britain, women are increasingly dissatisfied with work. A recent study by the University of Bath of female workers between 1992 and 2003 showed an overall decline in their stated levels of job satisfaction. For full-time female managers the decline was an above-average 6%. For men, job satisfaction over the same period went up.

The only category of female workers with a significant rise in satisfaction (of 19%) was that of part-time craft workers. It has become a lot more rewarding to blow glass or design gardens than to strive forever in a vain bid to reach the boardroom.

Change Needed

Will time alone erode the gap between men and women? The steep decline among women in the popularity of MBA degrees, the *sine qua non* [indispensable element] (at least in America) of a fast-track corporate career, suggests not. What is more, women with MBAs are fast dropping out of the workforce. One study in America found that one out of every three such qualified women is not working full-time. For men, the comparable figure is one in 20.

What can be done to improve the gender balance at the top? In Norway, legislation has been passed decreeing that by the end of 2006 all companies must have at least two women on their boards. Norway already leads the world in the number of women on its company boards

In Britain a group of businesswomen has set up an organisation called WDOB, or Women Directors on Boards whose aim is "to change the face of UK plc." Jacey Graham, its director, hopes to see the almost static percentage of female executive directors in Britain more than double (to 10%) by 2010.

Specific Intervention

Ms. Graham says that such change "won't just happen." It needs specific intervention within companies—intervention that is led from the top. Opportunities for flexible working are particularly helpful in keeping women in the workforce. KPMG, one of the Big Four accounting firms, is aiming to double the percentage of its partners who are women (currently 13%). It says flexible working is a key measure to help it achieve this goal. Three-quarters of all requests for flexible working over the past 12 months have been from women.

Mentoring is also helpful. The WDOB has initiated a programme in which the chairmen and CEOs of 25 FTSE100 companies nave agreed to mentor women who have been identified from other companies among the group as having boardroom potential. "The sad thing," says Ms. Graham, "is that some companies could not find a woman to put forward for mentoring." Women are enthusiastic mentors of each other. Colleen Arnold, the general manager of IBM Europe, Middle East and Africa, mentors 27 people formally and more than 100 informally. "Mentoring," she says, "is penalty-free."

Chief executives are appointed by sub-committees of companies' boards, often advised by headhunters. More of them will be women when more members of the sub-committees are women and when fewer headhunters are old white men. As Catalyst's Ms. Lang puts it: "There are so many women qualified to be on boards who are out there, under the radar screen." Heidrick & Struggles, a firm of headhunters, says that boards may need to look beyond the top-management structures from which non-executive directors are usually drawn if they are "to increase markedly the ratio of female to male directors."

Some think the task is particularly urgent. Chris Clarke, the America-based CEO of Boyden, a firm of headhunters, and a visiting professor at Henley Management College in England, argues that women are superior to men at multitasking, team-building and communicating, which have become the essential skills for running a 21st-century corporation. Maria Wisniewska, who headed a Polish bank, Bank Pekao, and is an international adviser to the Conference Board, says: "The links between the rational and emotional parts of the brain are greater in women than in men. If so, and if leadership is about making links between emotion and intelligence, then maybe women are better at it than men."

> *"The glass ceiling and gender gap ideas cannot ever be tried theories because they do not exist."*

The Glass Ceiling Has Never Existed

Lindsay McNutt

In the following viewpoint freelance writer Lindsay McNutt argues that not only are women not affected by the glass ceiling, it never existed in the first place. She asserts that the real reason that women do not hold high-ranking corporate jobs is that they either do not have the right level of education or they choose not to take on the difficult challenges of running a big company. Furthermore, affirmative action policies and radical feminists groups have only held women back by discouraging them from taking responsibility for their own successes.

As you read, consider the following questions:

1. When did the concept of the glass ceiling come to the forefront of U.S. debate?

2. According to a study conducted by the AFL-CIO and the Institute for Women's Policy Research, how much on the dollar did women 50 and older earn compared to men?

Lindsay McNutt, "The Glass Ceiling: It Can't Be Shattered If It Doesn't Exist," *www.ifeminists.com*, December 17, 2002. Reproduced by permission.

3. The number of women in business increased by what percentage from 1987 to 1992?

"I am woman hear me roar in numbers too big to ignore. And I know too much to go an' pretending cause I've heard it all before and I've been down there on the floor. No one's ever going to keep me down again."

For a group that would never be kept down again, they are fully embracing the idea of the glass ceiling. Women who boast the pride of their feminist views are fast to use the glass ceiling or gender gap idea in order to explain why they can't get jobs or move ahead based on their own personal merit. The glass ceiling and gender gap ideas cannot ever be tried theories because they do not exist.

Faulty Perceptions

The idea of a glass ceiling that oppresses women is absurd for many reasons. Supporters of this idea say, glass is clear so those forced under this ceiling would probably not even notice, at first, they were under such a restriction. But, if they tried to go through the glass, they would see quickly that the ceiling prohibited any rise to higher levels. This analogy is their only defense offered as to why the ceiling exists. Supporters say that it is a clear case of discrimination, which can only be resolved through affirmative action. Therefore, they are justified by using immoral and unfair tactics, such as denying a higher qualified person admission into college, in order to attain their allegedly constructive goals.

The concept of the glass ceiling really came to the forefront in 1987 and it was a political issue. It made the democratic platform more personal. But, as is typical in politics, the spin doctors took control and have been making a big to-do about it ever since. There are a few basic facts to recognize. In the late 1980's not many women over 40 had a college education and even less had a master's degree in the area of business. On top of that, these women did not have corporate maturity or experience to be top level executives. Unfortunately for these corporate women, they were thrust into jobs they were not prepared for because organizations like the National Organization for Women [NOW] and the Feminist Majority Foundation [FMF]. They demanded 50-50 representation in all occupations, therefore forcing better-qualified men to look for jobs elsewhere. Men were more qualified in education and experience by a 10:1 ratio over women. Luckily men and women have reached a reasonable balance of power in most corporations, and "it will continue to result in a huge advantage for the United States in global competition, because our society will remain far ahead of other major industrialized nations in selecting the best people, whether male or female, to lead its industrial enterprises." Obviously, these women did not hit the glass ceiling.

A study conducted by the AFL-CIO and the Institute for Women's Policy Research found that women 50 and older who are still active in the work place earn $.74 for every dollar that a man makes doing the same job. What the study results don't tell is that these women had little or no college education whereas the men had college diplomas. Also, the study defined "same job" as only part time or full time work. Credible research would take into account demographics including age, education, experience and occupation.

The Glass Ceiling Commission was set up to break down the "barriers resulting from institutional and psychological practices, and limit the advancement and mobility opportunities of women." They work to identify the glass ceiling and promote advancement and employment opportunities for women in order to place them in occupations of responsibility. So, in other words, people who are more qualified and educated for a specific job might be denied that because a "repressed" woman applied for the same job. This not only happens in the work place, but in social and education settings too.

The Glass Ceiling Myth

Myth: The "Glass Ceiling" prevents women from holding top corporate jobs.

This myth has been hanging around since 1995 when the Glass Ceiling Commission found only 5 percent female senior managers at *Fortune* 1000 and *Fortune* 500 companies and assumed discrimination. Their finding was politically useful but statistically wrong. It was based on the number of women in the total labor force, rather than the number of women actually qualified through education and experience to hold top positions.

A further look would have disclosed that while only 11 percent of corporate boards included women in 1973, by 1998 women sat on the boards of 72 percent of major corporations. As women continue to move through the "pipeline," toward the positions that typically require an MBA and 25 years experience, and as women increase their numbers in previously male-dominated fields and professions, more and more women will continue to achieve senior management positions in business and other fields.

"Equal Pay Day 2001: Economic Choices for Women,"
Independent Women's Forum, www.iwf.com, April 3, 2001.

While the commission felt they had the right to try to attempt to place women in these executive positions, they did not bother trying to find why this occurred. "The Fact-Finding Report of the Glass Ceiling Commission was a report of the perceptions of women in the workplace, and did not attempt to connect the presence of high-ranking women executives to profitability for their corporations. [Historians Diana] Furchtgott-Roth and [Christine] Stolba provided a guide to the economic progress of women and, since 1985, the advocacy group Catalyst has issued over 30 excellent research reports on various aspects of progress for women, but none of them have addressed the issue of profitability with empirical evidence."

Affirmative Action

Affirmative action is the love child of the glass ceiling and gender gap ideals. "Lots of young women who come out of college and enter the workforce feel like they're equal. Then they notice young men speeding ahead of them or they face sex discrimination or run up against the glass ceiling," said Loretta Kane, vice president of Action at the National Organization for Women. This is her argument that affirmative action should be interjected in workplace settings. In essence, what she is saying is that these women who lag behind their male counterparts shouldn't feel the compulsion to work harder; they should have it handed to them on a silver plate.

They should be given special treatment because they are women. When affirmative action was created, a respectable goal was in mind, which was recognition of equality under the law. To the chagrin of those who lobbied for it, it now embodies the idea of desiring equality of opportunity. Better yet, it is not affirmative action's job to monitor the ethical choices of business owners. If they choose to be sexist or racist, then that is their right. Affirmative action attempts to curtail violations of property rights. Governmental function is not to promise ethical choices, but to make sure no one's rights are infringed upon.

Furthermore, Christine Stolba, author of *Women's Figures: An Illustrated Guide to the Economic Progress of Women in America* feels that women have come far enough and that affirmative action is no longer necessary. She also believes that the Equal Employment Opportunity Commission (EEOC) is enough to ensure that discrimination is never a factor in employment issues. Her main concern though is, "Affirmative action undermines women's sense of self-worth. It has the effect of making women question their own success and other people questioning their success if they think they're just getting a leg up."

Currently, women make up 46% of the labor force, have raised their salary by $.15 in three decades and 37% of U.S. businesses are operated and owned by women. Also, out of all the taxpayer funded contracts that were given out, 5% of them went to women-owned business. This is up from 2.4% in just five years. Obviously the glass ceiling has not stopped these women from succeeding in their business endeavors.

Women's Decisions

Does prejudice exist? Should affirmative action continue to be standard which women rely on for a job? Or did it ever occur to anyone that maybe these women accept these standards because of American society? There are feminists who say that this glass ceiling and under-representation of women is because of a conscious coup to keep women out of executive offices. The more logical critics think that it's a subconscious prejudice that is introduced by our patriarchal society. Being a CEO or holding other executive offices requires a lot of responsibility, time away from home and takes precedence in the life of that individual. In American society, men are more willing to commit themselves to the meticulous schedule required by this job. There is a depressingly low number of women who apply for these jobs, so even if there were no prejudice, the result we see today would be duplicated. For example, nursing is traditionally a female dominated profession. Nurses have the potential to earn a tremendous amount of money if they work full time. Yet, many of these women voluntarily look for and take part-time positions. This not only lowers the average income earned by these women, but it also cuts the full-time job opportunity for nurses in half. Why? They want to raise their children, enjoy leisure activities or prefer for their husbands to work full time.

On the whole, because of the way the corporate world works, women are at a disadvantage. Males are almost inborn with the team spirit attitude and the military chain of command ideals. Also, women work less total hours than men, work fewer years, have less experience, and avoid dangerous jobs that accumulate a higher salary. There are feminists who focus on wages and promotions as the measure of how successful women are in society. They don't realize that there are women who are happy being homemakers and the economic importance of being a homemaker. If they acknowledged this, it would undermine the whole mission of their cause, which is to prove that women are forced to be homemakers because they can't land jobs in corporate America.

There are women who have accepted this role in American society. While they believe in the glass ceiling concept, they don't fully embrace the idea of it. They realize that in some degree, they are the substantive impetus. . . .

There will always be prejudice in business, education and society. But there is no reason to dream up these male-led conspiracies that are aimed at denying women chances for advancement. Because our society is imperfect, there will always be discrimination. But those businesses that continue to hire only "home-town boys" will eventually find themselves at a huge disadvantage because their rivals promote the competent females who do the same work. What's most important though is that no right exists to a job or college. Affirmative action abhors this basic fact. Proponents want women to sue, lobby and protest what they perceive as discrimination. . . .

Other options include create a business where women executives are welcomed. The use of force, the tactic so well used by the feminist groups such as NOW, is always wrong. Prejudice grows stronger only when the "well-intentioned" individuals who are against it use the very same tactics themselves.

The Gender Gap

[Social researcher] Dr. Pamela Edwards addressed the gender gap as concurring with a generation gap, which began in the 1960's. She felt though both genders shared similarities in the generation gap, there were specific differences between the roles they were keyed to play. According to Dr. Edwards, "Both genders rejected their parents, criticized materialism, criticized parents' world view, feared nuclear detonation, denounced anticommunism and condemned racism and poverty." Males or sons, "rejected adult society, still wanted fatherhood and marriage, and found success in their chosen career path." Females or daughters, on the other hand, feared "claustrophobic marriage, coercive motherhood, constrained chastity and a personal experience with the feminine mystique." They feared being an ordinary housewife which fueled the gender gap. If this was true, women fearing marriage and forced motherhood, then why was there a "baby bridge" in the 1970's when these sons and daughters became of the age to marry and have children? These are also the people who were the model yuppies and were the [former president Ronald] Reagan supporters.

Today's women are subjected to the same language that today's feminists were in their impressionable years. The difference is that today there are facts to prove that the gender gap really is just a non-existent excuse for one's lacking of personal merit. While the popular belief is still that women are restrained by a glass ceiling, a new study proves that women are not systematically discriminated against in the workforce. Women earn 95% to 98% as much as men when all the demographic characteristics are the same. From 1987 to 1992 the amount of women in business increased 43%. Out of those who are earning their associate, bachelor or master's degree, the large majority is women and 40% of doctorial candidates are female.

"The number of women in law school has risen dramatically in the last 30 years—from 8 percent in 1970, to 49.4 percent in the fall of 2000, and as of March 2001, the number of women applying to law schools surpassed men. In the country's most selective law schools, including Yale, Columbia and New York University, women have already passed the 50 percent mark. As the number of women with law degrees increases, women will be able to move into upper-level, higher-power positions in business and politics and the justice system."

In the last 10 years, the number of females in executive offices doubled. It can be safely determined that women no longer need affirmative action. . . .

In reality, the idea of the glass ceiling and gender gap are the concepts [of] those [feminists] like Gloria Stein[em] and Betty Freidan. "Women of today do not have time to deal with the fictional idea of an invisible barrier preventing them from excelling in corporate America." Many women now in the business mainstream have little or no interest in activist groups such as the National Organization for Women. N.O.W. pursued largely left-of-center political and social agendas in the past, but critics say its goals have now become irrelevant. The big concerns at their recent national convention were pushing the Susan B. Anthony dollar coin, bashing the Christian men's group Promise Keepers, and pushing for the rights of "transgender people," which could be anything from hermaphrodites to people waiting for sex change operations.

The feminist groups, such as NOW and the Feminist Majority Foundation have even gone as far as to blame Barbie for perpetuating and expanding the glass ceiling and gender gap.

"The doll has long been a touchstone in the wars over body politics. She was built to the dimensions of a male fantasy, and then sold to little girls eager to grow up and emulate her. Consequently, she has drawn the ire of two generations of feminists who, despite Barbie's reincarnations as a doctor, astronaut and presidential candidate, have blamed the doll for everything from anorexia to a plummeting of girls' self-esteem."

Their resorting to such absurd tactics shows they realize that not only is their grip slipping on the remaining feminists, but that they are becoming unable to convert the younger generation of girls. . . .

Women have been accepted into the job market, college educational settings and as vital parts of society. The only glass ceiling that might have existed before was one that women had put up themselves by measures like affirmative action and extreme feminist groups. The only way to break the glass ceiling is keep striking harder and harder, but you have to strike with the fragments of the extreme groups that need to be dismantled.

"We must zealously affirm women's right to assume leadership roles within the church."

Women Can Be Religious Leaders

Tony Campolo

Tony Campolo is professor emeritus of sociology at Eastern University in Pennsylvania, president and founder of the Evangelical Association for the Promotion of Education, and author of more than thirty books. In the following viewpoint, he argues that women can serve as religious leaders. Citing examples from the Bible, he asserts that Jesus was a radical feminist who would support women in such positions. Also, Campolo argues that it would be detrimental to keep women from the pulpit because their talents are desperately needed.

As you read, consider the following questions:

1. According to the author, why can it be concluded that Jesus was a radical feminist?

2. According to the author, in what ways has Evangelical Christianity supported feminists in the past?

3. Why is the author committed to supporting women's rights to be preachers and religious leaders?

I want to tell you something vitally important that is too often hidden from Evangelicals: Jesus was a radical feminist! Although it was common in his time to relegate women to a position inferior to men's, Jesus treated them as equals. He invited them to be students of the Torah, which back then was a privilege reserved for men (Matthew 10:35–42). He broke the taboo on touching women when they were menstruating (Mark 5:25–34). He was even willing to transgress ancient Jewish standards of social respectability by establishing relationships with women of questionable ethnic and moral backgrounds (John 4:1–27).

Women and the Bible

The Scripture tells us that "in Christ there is neither male nor female" and that "all are one in Christ Jesus" (Galatians 3:28). Nevertheless, many feminists get nervous around Evangelical Christians, and for good reason. They never know what to expect when they meet us. Some, like Mary Stewart Van Leeuwen, my colleague at Eastern University, are powerful advocates for women's equality. She and other Evangelical feminists provide convincing biblical support for the claim that Jesus opposed any form of second-class citizenship for women.

But other Evangelicals tend toward a version of Fundamentalism that legitimates the submission of women and leads them to oppose the idea of women's occupying leadership roles within the church. This latter group also relies on Scripture and readily quotes the apostle Paul in Ephesians 5:22–25:

> Wives, submit yourselves unto your own husbands, as unto the Lord. For the husband is the head of the wife, even as Christ is the head of the church: and he is the savior of the body. Therefore as the church is subject unto Christ, so let

the wives be to their own husbands in every thing. Husbands, love your wives, even as Christ also loved the church, and gave himself up for it.

and 1 Timothy 2:11–12:

Let the woman learn in silence with all subjection. But I suffer not a woman to teach, nor to usurp authority over the man, but to be in silence.

We believe that the Bible is infallible, and some Evangelicals take this to mean that in light of passages such as the ones I've quoted above, there is no wiggle room when it comes to defining the role of women in the home and in the church. But many of us disagree with this logic. The fact that the Bible is infallible does not mean that we have to take every passage of Scripture at face value. That may sound like heresy to most Fundamentalists, but some Evangelicals contend that, in interpreting Scripture, not every verse should be taken literally and certain rules of interpretation should be followed. One primary rule is that we should ask what any given passage meant to the people in the early church who first heard the words.

How, then, do we read these passages? Many Evangelicals cite church historians in explaining that these verses reflect Paul's response to a particular problem that had arisen among first-century Christians. Some Evangelical scholars suggest that some women who became Christians in the early days of the church were quick to abuse the new freedom and equality that they experienced as a product of their spiritual liberation. Some accounts indicate that some women, suddenly allowed to speak out and voice their concerns in religious gatherings, used the opportunity to discuss the ways in which their husbands were failing in their marital responsibilities. Some women, it is conjectured, even lectured their husbands in front of the entire congregation of fellow believers. If that was the case, it is easy to understand why Paul would tell them to

Women Ministers in Christian Churches

- There are almost 4,000 licensed and ordained women in the Assemblies of God.

- There are 1,225 ordained Southern Baptist women.

- The United Methodist Church has ordained women since 1956 and today has 4,743 women clergy.

- The Presbyterian Church (U.S.A.) has 2,419 female leaders.

- The United Church of Christ has 1,803 female leaders.

- The Evangelical Lutheran Church in America has 1,358 ordained women.

- As of 1994, 16 of the 30 independent Anglican communions around the world have approved ordination of women priests.

- The Church of Scotland approved the ordination of women in 1968 and now has 100 female ministers.

- Women now comprise at least a third of the student population at the leading interdenominational divinity schools; at Yale and Harvard, they're more than half.

"Women as Preachers," Way of Life Literature, www.wayoflife.org, May 11, 2002.

remain silent in church and enjoin them to talk to their husbands in the privacy of their homes (I Corinthians 14:34–35).

Wives Submitting to Husbands

What about wives submitting to their husbands? There are alternate ways of reading these lines as well. It seems clear to me that *mutual* submission is what is called for in Ephesians

5:22. In fact, many would [claim] that in the preceding verse, Paul calls upon husbands and wives to submit themselves to *one another* (Ephesians 5:21). Paul goes on to tell husbands to love their wives "even as Christ loved the church and gave himself up for it" (Ephesians 5:25). We know that Christ loved the church by becoming its servant (Philippians 2:7)—in the Greek language, the word is *doulos*, which means "slave." What wife would have any trouble submitting herself to a man who defined himself as her slave? And so, yes, wives are supposed to submit to their husbands, but Scripture also tells us that husbands should submit to their wives.

At this point, you may be asking, "Who, then, is the final authority in the decisionmaking process within the family?" The best answer to that question is "*Christ!*" Within biblical Christianity, husbands and wives are declared to be equals. When faced with difficult decisions, they should join together and prayerfully seek what Christ would have them do. According to Philippians 2:3, each partner should respect the opinions of the other and even give precedence to the other:

> Let nothing be done through strife or vainglory; but in lowliness of mind let each esteem the other better than themselves.

I have quoted several passages from Scripture in this letter because those Evangelicals who want to see women subordinated in both home and church constantly quote from Scripture to support their point of view. I want you to be well aware that their biblical case is not as strong as they claim that it is. One can use the very same passages and others to make a strong case for equality and mutuality between the sexes.

Not Always Antifeminist

Evangelicalism has not always been antifeminist. In fact, Evangelicals provided some of the most significant early support for the women's suffrage movement. As I mentioned in an earlier letter, Charles Finney, the acknowledged "Billy Graham" of the nineteenth century, made feminism a major part of his evangelistic preaching. He proved to be a leading recruiter of workers for the suffrage movement. Some of the earliest meetings of the feminist movement in America were held in Evangelical churches in upstate New York, in part as a result of Finney's preaching. Finney also believed that women should have leadership roles in the church. He played a major role in developing Oberlin Seminary and Oberlin College, where women were admitted to training courses to prepare them for Christian ministry.

Finney was doing nothing new or unprecedented when he advocated for women in ministry. According to Acts 2:18, God ordained women to prophesy (i.e., preach) from the earliest days of the church, when the Holy Spirit came upon the first-century Christians. We read in Scripture that the apostle Philip had daughters who preached (Acts 21:8–9) and about Euodia and Syntyche, who were leaders in the church at Philippi (Philippians 4:2). Women such as Priscilla played key teaching roles in the spiritual formation of male leaders (Acts 18:26). . . .

If we are going to change the minds of Evangelicals who use the Bible to try to suppress women, then we are going to have to use the Bible to make our case, too.

Christian Feminists

If you are wondering why I am so strongly committed to supporting women's right to be preachers and leaders, you should know that it is because of my mother. She had all the gifts to be a great preacher. I often watched her at family gatherings holding both young and old in rapt attention with her entertaining stories.

My mother always wanted to be a preacher, but back when she was coming of age, women were kept from taking that role. I am convinced that there is something horribly wrong with preventing someone like my mother from actualizing her

God-given gifts and living out her calling from God. Southern Baptists have made a major issue out of taking ordination away from women, and I believe that they are dead wrong. I believe that the Bible clearly teaches the doctrine of the "priesthood of all believers," which means that all Christians, regardless of gender, are ordained by God to all the callings of Christian ministry. I know that you two probably think that this is a no-brainer. It's not! Fundamentalists have made opposition to feminism a prominent part of their present-day agenda. You'll often hear their preachers refer to the feminist movement as being anti-Christian. Defining the family in a hierarchical fashion, with the husband as the head, they condemn any attempt to yield to wives equal authority.

These same Fundamentalists are threatened by anything that even *seems* like it is tending toward feminist thinking, as is evidenced by their upset over the use of inclusive language in church liturgy or in any translation of Scripture. You can count on their outrage in response to any suggestion that God transcends what some of us consider to be culturally prescribed definitions of masculinity. Whenever I preach about the mothering side of God—revealed, for instance, when Jesus talked about wanting to gather people together as a hen gathers her chicks (Matthew 23:37)—I can expect letters of condemnation during the days that follow.

Christian feminists believe that discovering the female side of God has made it easier for them to relate to God, but more important is the biblical case for affirming God's feminine traits. Consider the fact that when God's spirit is referred to in the Hebrew Bible, a feminine noun is used, and in the original Greek version of the New Testament, the Holy Spirit can be understood as being feminine.

We must zealously affirm women's right to assume leadership roles within the church. These roles were accorded to women in New Testament times, and they should be accorded to them now. We must support women's right to these roles not only because the cause is just, but also because we cannot afford to lose half of the talented people in the church as we embark on the tasks that lie before us in these crucial days. I beg you both to not let up in efforts to ensure women the opportunity to become all that they can be.

> "If a woman goes on serving as an elder or pastor, I believe she is doing so outside the will of God."

Women Cannot Be Religious Leaders

Wayne Grudem

Wayne Grudem is research professor of Bible and Theology at Phoenix Seminary in Scottsdale, Arizona, president of the Evangelical Theological Society, and the author of many books. In the following viewpoint he argues that women are not authorized to serve as leaders in Christian churches by pointing to scriptural and historical examples. He asserts that while women praying is always a positive act, women preaching from the pulpit is not acceptable to God and causes the feminization of both home and church.

As you read, consider the following questions:

1. What is one example of God extolling a blessing in spite of disobedience?

2. According to the author, the largest and most successful ministries in the United States are headed by preachers of which gender?

3. According to the author, how should women's roles in the church be determined?

Cindy Jacobs makes this argument [in *Women of Destiny*]:

> Women in numerous different ministries teach both men and women and are producing godly, lasting fruit for the Kingdom. Would that be happening if their work wasn't sanctioned by God? Wouldn't their ministries simply be dead and lifeless if God weren't anointing them?

In personal conversation, people will sometimes say, "I heard Anne Graham Lotz preach, and it changed my mind about women preaching." Or they will hear Beth Moore preach at a conference and think, *This is such good Bible teaching, how can it be wrong?*

But is this reasoning true? Does the evident blessing of God on some pastors prove that what they are doing is right?

Answer #1:

Of course there will be some good results when a woman prays, trusts God, and teaches God's Word, because God's Word has power and because God in His grace often blesses us in spite of our mistakes. But that does not make the mistakes right, and God may withdraw His protection and blessing at any time.

It is not surprising to me that there is some measure of blessing when women act as pastors and teach the Word of God, whether in a local congregation, at a Bible conference, or before a television audience. This is because God's Word is powerful, and God brings blessing through His Word to those who hear it.

But the fact that God blesses the preaching of His Word does not make it right for a woman to be the preacher. God is

Women Cannot Be Priests

According to the *Catechism of the Catholic Church*: "Only a baptized man (vir) validly receives sacred ordination." The Lord Jesus chose men (viri) to form the college of the twelve apostles, and the apostles did the same when they chose collaborators to succeed them in their ministry. The college of bishops, with whom the priests are united in the priesthood, makes the college of the twelve an ever-present and ever-active reality until Christ's return. The Church recognizes herself to be bound by this choice made by the Lord himself. For this reason the ordination of women is not possible.

Catechism of the Catholic Church: Second Edition.
New York: Doubleday, 2003.

a God of grace, and there are many times when He blesses His people even when they disobey Him.

One example where God brought blessing in spite of disobedience is the story of Samson in Judges 13–16. Even though Samson broke God's laws by taking a Philistine wife (Judges 14), sleeping with a prostitute at Gaza (Judges 16:1–3), and living with Delilah, a foreign woman he had not married (Judges 16:4–22), God still empowered him mightily to defeat the Philistines again and again. This does not mean that Samson's sin was right in God's sight, but only that God in His grace empowered Samson *in spite of his disobedience.* Eventually God's protection and power were withdrawn, "but he did not know that the Lord had left him" (Judges 16:20), and the Philistines captured and imprisoned him (v. 21).

If God waited until Christians were perfect before He brought blessing to their ministries, there would be no blessing on any ministry in this life! God's grace is given to us in spite of our failings. But that does not mean that it is right to disobey Scripture or that God will always give such blessing.

If a woman goes on serving as an elder or pastor, I believe she is doing so outside the will of God, and she has no guarantee of God's protection on her life. By continuing to act in ways contrary to Scripture, she puts herself spiritually in a dangerous position. I expect that eventually even the measure of blessing God has allowed on her ministry will be withdrawn (though I cannot presume that this will be true in every case).

Answer #2:

Arguments from the experience of blessing can go both ways: For two thousand years God has evidently blessed the ministries of millions of churches that have had only men as pastors and elders. Who are we to oppose what God has so clearly blessed?

Arguments based on experience are seldom conclusive. Even today, in the strongly egalitarian popular culture of the United States, by far the largest and most successful ministries (by any measure), the ministries that seem to have been most blessed by God, have men as senior pastors. Even those few large evangelical churches that have women as part of their pastoral team (such as Willow Creek Community Church) have a man (such as Bill Hybels) as the senior pastor, and men do most of the preaching. And evangelical churches with women pastors are few in comparison to the large number of churches that have only men as pastors and elders.

This fact should not be lightly dismissed. If it really were God's ideal for men and women to share equally in eldership and pastoral leadership roles, then at some point in the last two thousand years, and especially today, would we not expect to see a remarkable and unmistakable blessing of God on many churches that have an equal number of men and women as elders and that share the main Bible teaching responsibilities equally between men and women pastors?

And if the gender of pastors makes no difference to God, then why have we never seen God's evident blessing poured out abundantly on a church with *all women* pastors even once throughout the millions of churches that have existed in the last two thousand years?

Answer #3:

Liberal denominations that ordain women pastors have continually declined in membership and income.

Historian Ruth Tucker summarizes this trend [in *Women in the Maze*:

> The role of women in the church in the twentieth century will perplex future historians.... Those historians who dig deeper will discover that the mainline churches that were offering women the greatest opportunities were simultaneously declining in membership and influence. Some of these churches, which once had stood firm on the historic orthodox faith, were becoming too sophisticated to take the Bible at face value. The gains that have been made, then, are mixed at best.

Answer #4:

Having women as pastors or elders erodes male leadership and brings increasing feminization of both the home and the church. It also erodes the authority of Scripture because people see it being disobeyed.

When people say there is "much blessing" from the ministries of women pastors, I do not think they are able to see all the consequences. Once a woman pastor and woman elders are installed in a church, several other consequences will follow:

1. Many of the most conservative, faithful, Bible-believing members of the church will leave, convinced that the church is disobeying Scripture and that they cannot in good conscience support it any longer.

2. Some of those who stay will still believe that the Bible teaches that women should not be elders, but they will support the leadership of the church. Many of them will think that the leaders they respect are encouraging a practice of disobedience to Scripture, and this will tend to erode people's confidence in Scripture in other areas as well. . . .

3. A church with female elders or pastors will tend to become more and more "feminized" [Leon Podles, *The Church Impotent*] over time, with women holding most of the major leadership positions and men constituting a smaller and smaller percentage of the congregation.

4. Male leadership in the home will also be eroded, for people will reason instinctively if not explicitly that if women can function as leaders in the family of God, the church, then why should women not be able to function as well as men in leadership roles in the home? This influence will not be sudden or immediate, but will increase over time.

All this is to say that the "evident blessing" God gives when women preach the Bible is not the only result of such preaching. There are significant negative consequences as well.

Answer #5:

What is right and wrong must be determined by the Bible, not by our experiences or our evaluation of the results of certain actions.

Determining right and wrong by means of results is often known as "the end justifies the means." It is a dangerous approach to take in ethical decisions because it so easily encourages disobedience to Scripture.

In 1966, Joseph Fletcher published *Situation Ethics: The New Morality.* He argued that people at times needed to break God's moral laws in the Bible in order to do the greatest good for the greatest number of people. But as these ideas worked their way through American society, the "new morality" of Fletcher's situation ethics brought about a tremendous erosion of moral standards and widespread disobedience to all of God's moral laws.

If I say that women should be pastors because it brings good results, *even if the Bible says otherwise*, then I have simply capitulated to situation ethics. What is right and wrong must be determined by the teachings of Scripture, not by looking at the results of actions that violate Scripture and then saying those actions are right.

Answer #6:

Determining right and wrong on the basis of human experience alone is the foundation of liberalism in theology. Feminism takes us in that direction.

J. I. Packer explains [in "Liberalism and Conservatism in Theology" from *New Dictionary of Theology*that one of the characteristics of theological liberalism is "an optimistic view of cultured humanity's power to perceive God by reflecting on its experience." Thus, *experience* rather than the Bible becomes the ultimate standard in theology. If we decide that women and men can have all the same roles in the church primarily because we have seen blessing on the work of women preachers and Bible teachers, such an egalitarian argument leads us toward theological liberalism.

> "The time is right to blast through the armored ceiling that keeps women second-class citizens in the military."

Women Should Be Allowed to Serve in Combat

Robin Gerber

In the following viewpoint Robin Gerber argues that women should be permitted to serve in military combat. She asserts that restricting women from combat roles reduces their options for promotions in higher command positions. Gerber refutes a number of the arguments commonly given for keeping women out of combat by citing historical research and anecdotal evidence from real women's lives. Gerber is a senior scholar at the James McGregor Burns Academy of Leadership at the University of Maryland and the author of Leadership: The Eleanor Roosevelt Way.

As you read, consider the following questions:

1. What two reforms were made during the Clinton administration regarding women's service in the military?
2. What percentage of the positions in the Army and Marines are closed to women?

3. Who were the two women POWs captured during 1991's Desert Storm?

During the daring rescue of prisoner of war Jessica Lynch from an Iraqi hospital, the first commando to reach Lynch identified himself as a United States soldier. The 19-year-old Army private replied, "I'm an American soldier, too." [Lynch testified before Congress on April 24, 2007, that media coverage of her capture and rescue was fabricated.]

Lynch is a soldier—one who reportedly fought her abusive captors with heroism and courage—but she's a symbol, too. Her experience shows that the time is right to blast through the armored ceiling that keeps women second-class citizens in, the military.

Exclusions Remain

You might think, if you watch Operation Iraqi Freedom on TV or read about it in the newspaper, that the military already has been fully integrated with regard to gender. But you would be wrong.

Yes, progress has been made. Reforms during the Clinton administration in 1994 opened more than 250,000 positions to women in the armed services and allowed women to become fighter pilots and serve in most aviation specialties. In fact, Capt. Jennifer Wilson recently became the first woman to fly a B-2 in a combat mission.

But greater opportunity isn't equal opportunity. More than one-third of positions in the Army and Marines are closed to women. They cannot serve as front-line combat soldiers on the ground. Nor can women be members of the Special Forces. And the Navy still excludes women from serving on submarines.

In a Catch-22 way, these exclusions deny women opportunities for leadership, limiting chances for command positions. For instance, women can't interact with infantry and armor units as part of field-artillery command because of the bar on ground-combat participation. But ground combat is the kind of command that enhances career opportunities.

So what could the rationale be for maintaining a lid on how American women serve their country, for keeping all but a few women from achieving the highest ranks of the military?

Professor Mady Wechsler Segal, associate director of the Center for Research on Military Organization at the University of Maryland, has been doing research on women in the military for 30 years. "The arguments supporting the exclusion of women from ground combat that are used by those in the military and by civilians haven't changed," she says. "They are part of the public discourse and were used in the past to exclude women from jobs that they are now holding and performing well in."

A 1992 presidential commission used many of those well-worn arguments to push to maintain the status quo for women at the time. These dated excuses, as Lynch and many others before her have shown, no longer hold water.

Excuse No. 1:

Women lack courage and mental toughness. Lynch is only the latest in a long line of women who prove their sex's capacity for steely heroism. . . .

She emptied her rifle into Iraqi troops. It also has been reported that Pfc. Lori Piestewa, who died in the battle, fought with similar bravery. Gary Tuchman of CNN recently interviewed a woman identified only as Capt. KC (Killer Chick), an A-10 Warthog pilot. After taking heavy enemy fire over Baghdad, she landed the A-10 using the manual backup system. Was she afraid? "That's our job," KC told Tuchman. "We're here to help the guys out on the ground, and when they need our help, we're there." That's courage in my book.

Women in Combat in Iraq

Jennifer Guay went to war to be a grunt. And the 170-pound former bartender from Leeds, Maine, with cropped red hair and a penchant for the bench press, has come pretty close.

It was mid-February and Guay, 26, an Army specialist who was the first woman to be assigned as an infantry combat medic, was spending 10 hours a day on missions with the 82nd Airborne Division, dodging rockets and grenades in the crowded streets of Mosul. . . .

Day after day, Guay has faced situations that would test the steel of any soldier. And female soldiers like her—as well as Army officers who support them—are seizing opportunities amid Iraq's indiscriminate violence to push back the barriers against women in combat. As American women in uniform patrol bomb-ridden highways, stand duty at checkpoints shouldering M-16s and raid houses in insurgent-contested towns, many have come to believe this 360-degree war has rendered obsolete a decade-old Pentagon policy barring them from serving with ground combat battalions.

"The Army has to understand the regulation that says women can't be placed in direct fire situations is archaic and not attainable," said Lt. Col. Cheri Provancha, commander of a Stryker Brigade support battalion in Mosul, who decided to bend Army rules and allow Guay to serve as a medic for an infantry company of the 82nd Airborne. . . .

"This war has proven that we need to revisit the policy, because they are out there doing it," Provancha, a 21-year Army veteran from San Diego, said from her base in what soldiers call Mosul's "mortar alley." "We are embedded with the enemy."

Ann Scott Tyson, "For Female GIs, Combat Is a Fact,"
Washington Post, May 13, 2005.

In *They Fought Like Demons*, authors DeAnne Blanton and Lauren Cook tell the stories of hundreds of female soldiers during the Civil War who hid their gender in order to fight. How much mental toughness did that take? Outside of the military, women serve as firefighters, police officers and emergency workers. Try telling them or the communities they serve that they lack the right stuff.

Excuse No. 2:

Women have an adverse effect on male bonding and cohesion in a unit.

Lynch proved not only that she was able to fight to defend her unit, but also that she was part of a group in which everyone was fighting to protect each other.

On her Web site devoted to women in the military, retired Air Force captain Barbara Wilson has many stories of gender-integrated units that worked well together. Julie Tovsen, a Desert Storm veteran, wrote that she served with "30 men in my platoon who respected me and bonded in a way beyond gender. . . . We learned a lesson that I hope to keep for the rest of my life—that people are what is important. It was understood that I would be there for them as they were there for me."

Excuse No. 3:

Women lack the physical strength needed far ground combat.

This is true of some women—and some men. No one is arguing that anyone in the military should be assigned beyond their capabilities, or that standards should be lowered for the infantry. But there is ample evidence that there are women who can meet the physical requirements for ground combat. Generalizing physical attributes to all women is as discriminatory an action as generalizing physical attributes by race.

Excuse No. 4:

Captured women possibly will be raped. Every soldier understands that becoming a POW means the possibility of abuse and torture. As the experiences of Lynch and Spec. Shoshana Johnson underscore, keeping women out of combat positions—both were with the 507th Maintenance Company when captured—does not protect them from becoming POWs and possibly facing this danger.

In 1991's Desert Storm, two women also were POWs: Army flight surgeon Maj. Rhonda Cornum and Army Transportation Spc. Melissa Rathbun-Nealy. Cornum, who suffered multiple injuries when the helicopter carrying her was shot down, was sexually assaulted and repeatedly interrogated. As she told *Time* magazine, "You're supposed to look at this as a fate worse than death. Having faced both, I can tell you it's not. Getting molested was not the biggest deal of my life."

Rape, of course, is not a torture restricted by gender, nor is the determination to withstand whatever the enemy dishes out. "The qualities that are most important in all military jobs, things like integrity, moral courage and determination, have nothing to do with gender," Cornum has said.

Change Is Necessary

It's time to end the excuses and face the reality of modern warfare where the combat front has been redefined. Supply lines stretch over miles; guerrilla fighting from the enemy is expected behavior. The female MPs searching under full-length abayas, where women in Afghanistan hide AK-47s, are risking their lives as surely as the ground troops storming the streets in Baghdad.

They are all American soldiers, as Lynch reminded us.

The young private from West Virginia is likely to receive a medal for her heroism. But the best tribute to her and all other female soldiers past and present will be to remove the last barriers to equal opportunity for women in the armed services.

> *"There are substantial physical differences between men and women that place the latter at a distinct disadvantage when it comes to ground combat."*

Women Should Not Be Allowed to Serve in Combat

Mackubin Thomas Owens

Mackubin Thomas Owens is associate dean of Academics for Electives and Directed Research and professor of Strategy and Force Planning at the U.S. Naval War College in Newport, Rhode Island. In the following viewpoint he expresses his concern about recent Army violations of the regulations prohibiting women from engaging in ground combat. He asserts that the military should continue to ban women from ground combat because of women's physical limitations, interpersonal issues related to gender differences, and the potential impact on morale and performance due to the presence of women on the battlefield.

As you read, consider the following questions:

1. In 1994, then-secretary of defense Les Aspin issued what regulations regarding women in the military?

Mackubin Thomas Owens, "A Man's Job," *National Review Online*, May 12, 2005. Copyright © 2005 by National Review, Inc., 215 Lexington Avenue, New York, NY 10016. Reproduced by permission.

2. According to the author, how has the Army created a new regulation regarding women in combat that has not been authorized by the secretary of defense?
3. According to the author, why is pulling women out of their units at the last minute before battle a problem?

On May 11, [2005] the Subcommittee on Military Personnel of the House Armed Services Committee approved legislation requiring the Army to prohibit women from serving in any company-size unit that provides support to combat battalions or their subordinate companies. This is in no way revolutionary. In fact, as I wrote in *National Review* in December 2004, the House panel is merely telling the Army to abide by existing regulations.

In the late 1980s and early 1990s, the U.S. military opened a number of specialties to women. Changes in regulations permitted women to serve on the Navy's combatant ships and fly Navy and Air Force combat aircraft. Ground combat, however, was still closed to them.

One of the reasons for these changes was the widespread acceptance of the view that technological advances had created a "revolution in military affairs" (RMA). Many of the more vociferous RMA promoters argued that emerging technologies had so completely changed the nature of war as to render the old verities that underpinned the traditional military ethos no longer true. RMA advocates contended that these emerging technologies and "information dominance" would eliminate "friction" and the "fog of war," providing the commander and his subordinates nearly perfect "situational awareness," thereby promising the capacity to use military force without the same risks as before. If this was the case, why did we need these old restrictions that merely hampered the progress of women? As former congresswoman Pat Schroeder famously remarked, a woman can push a button just as easily as a man.

Nonetheless, restrictions remained on women when it came to ground combat. On January 13, 1994, then-secretary of defense Les Aspin issued regulations prohibiting the assignment of women to units that engage in direct ground combat, e.g., infantry and armor. In his memo to the Services, Aspin said that "women should be excluded from assignment to units below the brigade level whose primary mission is to engage in direct combat on the ground," defined as "engaging an enemy on the ground with individual or crew-served weapons, while being exposed to hostile fire and to a high probability of direct physical contact with the hostile force's personnel." This prohibition extended to the support units that were collocated with direct ground combat forces as well.

Restrictions Violations

These regulations are still in effect. But the U.S. Army has violated these regulations without the notification required by current law, which requires the secretary of defense to provide formal advance notice to Congress of policy changes regarding female soldiers, accompanied by an analysis of proposed revisions on women's exemption from Selective Service obligations.

In an attempt to make its units more "expeditionary," the Army has developed a new concept that permits the deployment and employment of self-contained formations task organized for specific combat tasks. The 3rd Infantry Division, which recently redeployed to Iraq is the first Army unit to deploy to a combat zone under the new organizational concept.

The Army originally envisioned support troops as part of a self-contained "unit of action." But if a forward-support company (FSC) is part of a combat unit, current DoD policy says that it cannot include women. Claiming that there are not enough male soldiers to fill its FSCs, the Army moved the FSCs from the maneuver battalions into the "gender"-integrated brigade support battalions (BSBs). Of course no

Women are Not Physically Able to Serve in Combat

The advocates of women in combat say the front line is everywhere in Iraq. They continually try to fuzzy over the difference between being subject to risk (such as being ambushed by a car bomb) versus the task of aggressively seeking out and killing the enemy. . . .

Putting women in military combat is the cutting edge of the feminist goal to force us into an androgynous society. Feminists are determined to impose what Gloria Steinem called "liberation biology" that pretends all male-female differences are culturally imposed by a discriminatory patriarchy.

History offers no evidence for the proposition that the assignment of women to military combat jobs is the way to win wars, improve combat readiness, or promote national security.

Women, on the average, have only 60 percent of the physical strength of men, are about six inches shorter, and survive basic training only by the subterfuge of being graded on effort rather than on performance. These facts, self-evident to anyone who watches professional or Olympic sports competitions, are only some of the many sex differences confirmed by scholarly studies.

Denial of physical differences is an illusion that kills. That's the lesson of the Atlanta courtroom massacre where a 5-foot-one, 51-year-old grandmother police guard was overpowered by a 6-foot-tall, 210-pound former football linebacker criminal; so now three people are dead.

Phyllis Schlafly, "Women Don't Belong in Ground Combat,"
EagleForum.org, June 1, 2005.

matter where the FSCs appear on a table of organization, the fact is that in order to be effective, the soldiers of an FSC would have to live and work with the maneuver battalions all of the time.

As Elaine Donnelly [president of the Center for Military Readiness] has pointed out, the Army has apparently rewritten the regulations regarding women in such a way as to make Bill Clinton's infamous statement that "it depends on what the meaning of is, is," appear to be straightforward. In her May 8 [National Review Online] *NRO* piece describing a presentation by Army chief of staff General Peter Schoomaker at the American Enterprise Institute, she writes:

> Current directives exempt female soldiers from direct ground-combat units such as the infantry and armor, and from smaller support companies that "collocate" (operate 100 percent of the time) with land-combat troops. The new, unauthorized wording narrows the "collocation rule" to apply only when a combat unit is actually "*conducting* an assigned direct ground combat mission." (Emphasis added.)

General Schoomaker recited Defense Department [DoD] regulations, but claimed (without justification) that the Army has separate rules that exempt female soldiers from collocation with land-combat battalions "at the time that those units are *undergoing* those operations" (emphasis added). By adding the words "conducting" or "undergoing" (a direct ground-combat mission) to the collocation rule, the Army has created a new regulation that has not been authorized by the secretary of defense, or reported to Congress in advance, as required by law.

In other words, the Army says it is not in violation of DoD regulations because women in FSCs are not really "collocated" until the combat unit is engaged or about to be engaged in a direct combat mission. The breathtaking assumption here is that women in these units can be pulled out before the battle starts.

Women Should Not Serve

General Schoomaker is a very experienced and able soldier. He certainly understands the role of "friction" and the "fog of uncertainty" in battle, having experienced these phenomena first hand. He must know that trying to pull women out of their units under such circumstances, even if it could be done at all in the chaos and confusion of combat, would be incredibly disruptive, undermining unit cohesion and effectiveness and diverting resources needed to prevail in the battle.

Over the years, I have argued against the idea of placing American women in combat or in combat support or service support associated with direct ground combat. I base my position on the fact there are substantial physical differences between men and women that place the latter at a distinct disadvantage when it comes to ground combat. In addition, men treat women differently than they treat other men. This can undermine the comradeship upon which the unit cohesion necessary to success on the battlefield depends. The presence of women also leads to double standards that have a serious impact on morale and performance. In other words, men and women are not interchangeable. As I wrote in January, even the Israelis, who draft women into the [Israel Defense Forces] IDF, do not place them in ground combat units.

As persuasive as I believe my arguments are, the decision to place women in units that expose them to direct ground combat does not depend on my opinion. But it does not depend exclusively on the Army either. If the president and the secretary of defense believe the regulations should be changed to reflect the Army's new approach, the latter needs to advise Congress, as current law requires. As Donnelly observes, this is a national-security matter, not a less important "women's issue." As such, Congress needs a say in this matter.

Periodical Bibliography

The following articles have been selected to supplement the diverse views presented in this chapter.

Terry Castle	"Women's Empowerment," *Atlantic Monthly*, June 2006.
Elizabeth H. Gorman	"Work Uncertainty and the Promotion of Professional Women: The Case of Law Firm Partnership," *Social Forces*, December 2006.
Catherine Hakim	"Women, Careers, and Work-life Preferences," *British Journal of Guidance & Counselling*, August 2006.
Chris Jones	"The Change," *Esquire*, July 2006.
Lisa M. Keels	"Family and Medical Leave Act," *Georgetown Journal of Gender & the Law*, 2006.
Andrew Lawler	"Universities Urged to Improve Hiring and Advancement of Women," *Science*, September 22, 2006.
Maria Misra	"New Role Model: A Fogey in Tweed," *Times Higher Education Supplement*, February 2, 2007.
Louise North	"'Just a Little Bit of Cheeky Ribaldry'?" *Feminist Media Studies*, March 2007.
Catherine O'Connell-Cahill	"Working Without a Net," *U.S. Catholic*, January 2007.
Bruce L. Plopper	"Alice in Journalism," *Quill*, December 2006.
Anna Quindlen	"Everyday Equality," *Newsweek*, September 25, 2006.
Damaris Rose	"Working Feminism," *Environment & Planning D: Society & Space*, December 2006.
Working Mother	"Great Expectations," February–March 2007.

CHAPTER 4

How Has Feminism Affected Women's Roles in the Home?

Chapter Preface

Although women have finally gained some measure of respect and equality in the workplace, they continue to struggle to achieve the same balance at home. Despite changing societal attitudes about so-called women's work, it remains unusual for male partners to take on the majority or even half of household duties. While studies in the early 2000s reveal that there have been improvements in the amount of housework done by men, women, especially working women, are still stuck doing double shifts.

A 2002 University of Michigan study revealed that American men are doing more housework than ever before. According to the study, men are putting in 16 hours a week around the house, up from just 12 hours a week in 1965. Nevertheless, women still come in first for their share of domestic duties at 27 hours a week. Complicating this issue are the perceptions that both men and women feel about their contributions to the household. A 2005 study published in the *Journal of Marriage and Family* discovered that women believe that men only do about 33 percent of the housework, while men believe that they do 42 percent. In reality, evidence reveals that men do around 39 percent of household chores.

Perhaps perception is the most powerful factor in encouraging a more equal distribution of household labor. A study conducted by John Gottman of the University of Washington found that women are more likely to find their husbands to be sexually attractive if they did housework. Sociologist Scott Coltrane of the University of California at Riverside speculates that the reason women find men who share in the household duties sexually appealing is likely because the "wives may be less stressed over balancing work and home and that wives interpret husbands' domestic contributions as a sign of love and caring and are therefore more sexually attracted to their mates." No matter what the reason, Gottman's study does seem to ring true as evidenced by the success of *Porn for Women*, a book featuring photos of men in aprons engaged in a number of household duties, such as vacuuming, dusting, and ironing. According to the authors of the book, the Cambridge Women's Pornography Cooperative, "men who clean the bathroom without being asked, or make a gourmet dinner, or bring home flowers for no reason, or volunteer to watch the kids" are sexually enticing to women.

Of course, the real issue behind the quest to get men to do more work around the house is the overwhelming stress that most women are under today. Even stay-at-home mothers are swamped with endless tasks that mothers just generations before them did not have to take on, such as coordinating multiple busy after-school schedules. However, as some of the viewpoints in this chapter argue, some women believe that these stresses could easily be lifted if women made better life choices, such as putting their careers on hold to start families, marrying later in life, and staying home with their children.

"I just don't perceive the feminist and
pro-family viewpoints as complete opposites."

Feminists Can Be Pro-Family

Lynn Marcotte

*Lynn Marcotte is an assistant professor of English at Gordon
College in Wenham, Massachusetts, where she teaches writing
classes, oversees the Writing Center, and directs the Writing-
Across-the-Curriculum program. In the following viewpoint she
argues that it is possible for feminists to support family values.
She asserts that by discerning the most important features of
each philosophy women can find harmony in their lives. Furthermore, Marcotte notes, proponents of both sides should work together to understand what values they have in common and
unite under those goals.*

As you read, consider the following questions:

1. According to the author, what four values do both feminists and pro-family supporters have in common?
2. During what historical period did the ideal of the "traditional family" originate?
3. How does the American Home Economics Association
   define the family?

Lynn Marcotte, "Being Feminist and Pro-Family," *E-Quality*, fall 2005. www.cbeinter
national.org. Copyright © 2005. Reproduced by permission.

Like many women in the church today, I wear several hats: wife, mother, and professional. Even though I find support for those roles within my own church, I am discovering that my experience is rare and that what women and men should do about marriage, family, and work is a heated issue. There seem to be two camps vying for our allegiance today: the pro-family movement and feminism. And, according to some, a Christian can't be both pro-family *and* feminist.

The Main Issues

The issues look something like this: First, there's the pro-family movement, which is interested in supporting and sustaining the traditional family. It is thus committed to social and political issues related to the sustenance of the family because it thinks family life is being undermined and devalued. According to pro-family advocates, this deterioration is caused by such practices as widespread cohabitation, no-fault divorce, joint custody of children, blurred gender roles, government intrusion into the family, and the rampant growth of child-care centers. Many people who are active in the pro-family movement find a biblical basis for maintaining what they deem *traditional* family life and for fighting politically against its deterioration.

Then there is feminism. It believes that men and women should be treated as equals—socially, economically, and politically. Throughout history, women in a variety of cultures have been expected to submit to a prescribed set of behaviors, and as a result have suffered varying levels of mistreatment, both subtle and profound. Out of a deep frustration by what has historically happened to women and by what they presently experience, feminists are vocal, active, and adamant about change. The old system, the so-called traditional ways, cannot support equality of the sexes, so feminists are agitating for a new paradigm of human relationships. There's a deep fear of regression or minimal change, so they are fighting for sweeping change. They want a new paradigm.

This new paradigm, feminists say, could ultimately be freeing for both men and women. Like pro-family advocates, feminists have broadened the issues at stake. Not wanting to let government, society and men control them any longer, many women are demanding an environment where they have control over their bodies and their lives. So, inevitably, issues like abortion, birth control, divorce, day-care, and welfare benefits have come into the discussions. Like pro-family advocates, many feminists find a biblical basis for changing both society and the church.

Pros and Cons of Both Sides

I find it easy to get confused when I look at the agendas of both the pro-family movement and the feminist movement. Some of the things feminists often advocate, such as no-fault divorce laws or legalized abortion, are the very things pro-family advocates are alarmed about. Likewise, some of the things the pro-family movement seems to encourage, like a hierarchy dictated by gender, have the feminists disturbed.

As a wife and mother, I have little use for the traditional roles the pro-family movement thinks are so crucial to the health of family life. Neither does my husband. Yet, my husband and I are committed to making our home a healthy, stable place for our children and ourselves. We make decisions together, we are both equally responsible for our children's well being, and we both find we need work that gives us a sense of satisfaction and purpose.

In our own home, for example, my husband and I feel we should be the primary caregivers to our children, ages one and four, rather than turn them over all day to persons outside the home. As it has turned out, one of us is the primary breadwinner and one takes care of the children while the other works; to us it doesn't matter which one of us works or which one of us takes care of the kids. What we value is that we are the ones who are the most involved with our children. This may not work out for everyone, but it is our own vision for keeping our family healthy and intact.

If someone observed the way my husband and I function in our relationship and in our home, we look very "traditional" at times and we look very "feminist" at times. It depends on who is looking and when. This seems to be true for many Christian families. But the point is this: as we evaluate how best to nurture family life, we cannot be quick to judge and criticize those who may be doing a fine job, just because the way they do it may not look [like] the way we do it. That's not to say that we shouldn't be critical as Christians when we look at our culture and its values, or that we shouldn't be open to criticism and change. But we shouldn't be critical about the wrong things or too stubborn to change. . . .

When I look at my own life and the experiences of those in my church, I just don't perceive the feminist and pro-family viewpoints as complete opposites. In fact, I think they both ultimately want the same things: a healthy society where both men and women can live at their full potentials, where families find support and encouragement, where fidelity between husbands and wives is valued, and where bearing and raising children is valued. It has made me wonder what these movements have done to polarize each other so drastically and so weaken the important goals of each.

Understanding Feminism

One thing that has alienated me at times—and I sense has polarized many Christians—is "that word." Many believers, even though they practice mutuality of the sexes, are afraid to admit it or label it or be active in a movement for change in the church because they are afraid of "that word." They are afraid of being labeled and thus judged by the standards of "that word." Choosing between the two camps is a dilemma that faces many Christians, and to many it seems far more "spiritual" to be pro-family than *feminist* (ah, there, I named it). If we Christians can just overcome our fear of that word and embrace what we know God wants for both men and women, then we can actively and fervently be part of the transformation God is working in the church today.

A way to begin overcoming this fear is by understanding what feminism actually is. As one dictionary tells it, feminism is the theory of political, economic, and social equality of the sexes. For Christians, we can add spiritual equality. I think I would be hard pressed to find someone who didn't support those ideas. Feminism is also an organized activity on behalf of women's rights and interests. The second definition has come to be the sum total of feminism in many people's minds. And, this "feminism," along with the good it has produced, also carries with it an excess baggage of doctrine and reputation that many people hesitate to support.

I may not agree with everything that the different wings of the feminist movement have done or hope to do, but I don't have a problem sorting that out. We need to have an intelligent faith that is not afraid to look at the movement and trust the Holy Spirit to help us discern what is part of God's plan and what is not.

No Ideal Family

Likewise, I find that I can be pro-family without accepting lock, stock, and barrel everything the pro-family movement finds necessary to our well-being. It is possible to be pro-family and not support an archaic hierarchy of male/female roles.

This whole idea of the "traditional family" as an ideal has only existed since the Industrial Revolution. So to go back to a supposed ideal that was lived out for such a short period of time is not only historically inaccurate but is certainly biblically naive. It doesn't even attend to the economic realities of our lives.

201

"Inconvenient" Feminist History

Concepts like equality and issues like abortion have been actively debated within feminism since the movement's inception. The most cursory review of "inconvenient" feminist history reveals:

- Susan B. Anthony and Elizabeth Cady Stanton, two of the Founding Mothers of feminism, strongly opposed abortion. Victoria Woodhull, the first female presidential candidate, shared their opposition.

- Many 19th-century feminists did not advocate diversity but elitism and racism. Even Margaret Sanger, who is lauded for bringing birth control to immigrant women, argued that the world would be better off without "certain types" of children—namely, those who were "less fit." Some prominent 19th-century suffragists advocated adopting educational or property qualifications for voting that would disqualify most black women.

- Religion often constituted the backbone of belief for early feminists, many of whom were Quakers like Lucretia Mott who, along with Stanton, organized Seneca Falls—the first woman's rights convention in America. When Stanton herself blasted the impact of religion on women through "The Woman's Bible," the National American Woman Suffrage Association denounced the work.

My purpose in pointing to inconvenient history is not to slur the feminist past or to champion one position over another. It is to confirm that there has always been a wide range of opinion on key issues such as the role of abortion and religion in women's lives. And there always should be.

Wendy McElroy, "The Advent of Christian Feminism,"
www.ifeminists.com, September 2, 2003.

Most men and women work because they have to, so they can provide food, clothing, and shelter for their families. And it's not a glamorous life out there for the majority of workers. Women are not listlessly eating their chocolates, watching soap operas, and saying, "Oh this life's a bore, I think I'll find a job." The hard economic reality is that many women work because they must.

Yet, pro-family advocates insist that family life is doomed to a slow death unless we re-establish the male headship over the home and the female submission to that headship, which often means men must work and women must not. They insist that we will be blurring our sexual identity and the identity of our children if men and women can do the same activities, instead of doing a set of pre-ordained ones.

Both Sides Must Unite

Are feminists and pro-family advocates then part of separate camps, enemies to one another? Does the baggage they carry require that we choose one over the other?

Some say I am naive in thinking I can be part of both camps. Pro-family advocates insist that the many issues, from sexual identity to pro-life concerns and a narrow definition of family, are all related and biblically founded, and must all be embraced to save the family from deterioration. Likewise, feminists give the impression that for women and men to experience true equality we must support abortion on demand and re-define the family.

I believe that unless both camps realize they agree on some basic things and can acknowledge that certain values are crucial to all concerned, neither will be as successful as they would like in changing our culture. In fact, being both feminist and pro-family can look quite different from being only one or the other. We don't need to force an impossible agreement between the feminist and pro-family movements. Instead, we need to start by being critical in our thinking and realize that there are things on both sides that don't belong in a "pro-family/feminist movement." And, there are also some things that do. As we undergo this process, I believe we will be transformed into people who understand the evolution of the issues and show compassion toward the individuals who, to us, seem to overreact. As Christians, we should be most concerned with love, forgiveness, and compassion, rather than with dogmatic adherence to a set of lifeless regulations. That also holds true as we allow God to transform us into *being pro-family and feminist.*

To be people who are both pro-family and feminist means being *non-judgmental yet discerning.* It means, for example, understanding that something must be very wrong with society's treatment of women to put them in a predicament of having to use abortion as birth control. We may not support abortion on demand, but we can have a gentle spirit toward women faced with unwanted pregnancies. Instead of judging the victim, we should try to change society so that there are fewer victims. Actually, it has always seemed ironic to me that the feminist movement wants a humanized world with equal rights for all, yet it is adamant that the right of a woman to get an abortion overrides the right of the child she bears.

Redefining the Family

Those who are pro-family and feminist *value biblical principles of commitment and marriage, yet are compassionate* towards individuals in other lifestyles. We are alarmed by the soaring divorce rate, the lax acceptance of homosexuality and cohabitation, and the lack of commitment in today's marriages and families. Yet we are compassionate toward those struggling in their marriages, in their sexual identity, and in their attempts to redefine the family, where, in the words of the American Home Economics Association [AHEA] a family simply consists of "two or more persons who share values and goals, and have commitments to one another over time." Even college roommates would qualify under that watered-down definition. They certainly have common goals—a clean, cheap apartment—and commitments to one another over time—a lease until the end of the school year. Yet how many college roommates would consider theirs a "family" arrangement? In this re-definition, the AHEA is probably trying to recognize broken homes, varying types of blended families, gay marriages, and cohabitating individuals as alternative types of families. I don't have a problem recognizing the existence of some of these lifestyles, but I do have a hard time placing them side by side with what is ideal, and that is the committed, loving marriage between a woman and a man who may or may not bear and raise children.

The feminist movement's redefinition of family is a fair description of a reality in our society, but it should not replace the ideal institution of marriage and family, an ideal that respects lifelong commitment. Acknowledging the existence of less-than-ideal ways of doing things does not mean redefining our value system in order to make them exemplary. Even divorced individuals still value commitment and marriage. That's why divorce and remarriage can be such painful and complicated processes. They are not painful because our society doesn't condone them; they are painful because they go against the grain of how we are made, of what we know, deep in our being, to be true and right.

Gender Roles in Conflict

Finally, the feminist/pro-family individual *does not see a male-dominant hierarchy as part of healthy and biblical family life.* The pro-family movement has long been criticized for its dogmatic adherence to the "Father Knows Best" style of marriage and family, where, in the most extreme scenario, men are the ultimate authority and women merely act on their orders. Pro-family advocates fear that, if it is any other way, then we are both disobeying God's way and pushing for a genderless society. Men and women are different, but those differences don't mandate that only women or only men can do X, Y, or Z. Minimally, the differences mean that women physically bear children and men don't.

Here begins one of the biggest gray areas in these movements. As soon as we start enumerating what men and women can and can't do, we run the risk of squelching the Spirit of God at work in each individual. Sometimes women are better at nurturing than men. So what? Does that mean all women should stay home and raise their children and all men go to work all day? A major change I would like to see in society is one where it is equally acceptable for either men or women to work and equally acceptable for either men or women to stay home with the kids, if that is what they choose to do. How many men could quit their jobs midstream in their careers, stay home for several years to raise their children, and then reenter the work force as freely as they left it? They would not only get a few raised eyebrows if they tried, but they'd be criticized and most likely discriminated against as they tried to regain employment. On the other hand, women may not be able to freely reenter the work force either, but most likely they would experience a different kind of prejudice.

It's all to say that these issues are not as black and white as the pro-family advocates or feminists make them out to be. I consider myself very different from men and don't desire to live in a society where my sexual identity is blurred, but I just cannot live out the prescribed roles the pro-family advocates call "biblical" and "crucial to the health of society." Nor do I want admittance to the hierarchy of power that men have designed over the centuries. So where do I fit in?

I live *actively* with the ambiguity; I try to be intelligent and discerning in my faith, sorting out what's good from what's not so good. It is not easy to grapple with issues of gender roles and family life. Both pro-family advocates and the feminist movement have identified some real problems in our society, problems that deprive women and men of their wholeness, their humanness, and their gifts. . . .

*"Bounding home is not good for women
and it's not good for society."*

Mothers Should Work

Linda Hirshman

*Linda Hirshman is a retired philosophy and women's studies
professor of Brandeis University and the author of several books.
In the following viewpoint she argues that women's options for
life satisfaction are limited by gender-specific societal expectations. She is dismayed by the number of highly educated, successful women who stop working to stay at home to care for their
husbands and children. She asserts that women should not drop
out of the workplace because doing so re-establishes the unequal
distribution of domestic labor and decreases the influence that
women can have on the future of the nation.*

As you read, consider the following questions:

1. What percentage of housework is done by women?
2. According to the 2002 U.S. Census, what percentage of
   women with graduate degrees and children under one
   work full time? Part time?

Linda Hirshman, from *Get to Work: A Manifesto for Women of the World*. New York:
Viking, 2006. Copyright © Linda Hirshman, 2006. All rights reserved. Reproduced by
permission of Viking, a division of Penguin Putnam Books.

3. According to a survey by the Center for Work-Life Policy, what percentage of women with graduate degrees or prestigious bachelor's degrees had taken time out from work?

If Betty Friedan [author of *The Feminine Mystique*] had lived just a little longer. We are about to restart the revolution. But now we have to do it without her.

For twenty-five years, she watched as the backlash generation slowly walked away from the promise of a better life. Women—whether they stay home or, like most women, just carry the responsibility for home to work and back—are homeward bound. Their men won't carry enough of the household to enable them to succeed fully in the public world. Glass ceiling? The thickest glass ceiling is at home.

Their bosses, who are mostly someone else's husband, won't do the job their own husbands turned down, so there is no employer day care, and there are precious few government tax breaks. Look deeply and you will see that liberal and conservative commentators largely agree that ideally women belong at home.

And women say they choose this fate, and the feminist movement backs them up.

"Choice feminism," the shadowy remnant of the original movement, tells women that their choices, everyone's choices, the incredibly constrained "choices" they made, are good choices. . . .

Bounding home is not good for women and it's not good for the society. The women aren't using their capacities fully; their so-called free choice makes them unfree dependents on their husbands. Whether they leave the workplace altogether or just cut back their commitment, their talent and education are lost from the public world to the private world of laundry and kissing boo-boos. The abandonment of the public world by women at the top means the ruling class is overwhelmingly male. If the rulers are male, they will make mistakes that benefit males. Picture an all-male Supreme Court. We may well go back there. What will that mean for the women of America?

Educated women opting out and working mothers throughout society doing 60 percent to 70 percent of the housework reveals a hard truth. Good economic research shows that women have squeezed as much out of their days as they can without more help. For all its achievements, feminism cannot make more progress, private or public, until it turns its spotlight on the family. Child care and housekeeping have satisfying moments but are not occupations likely to produce a flourishing life. Gender ideology places these tasks on women's backs; women must demand redistribution. . . .

At this moment, 55 percent of college undergraduates are female—girls who should have a vision and wish to shape the future to it, to aspire to something complex and demanding, which they know they can do well—become a great artist or a crusading prosecutor, own their own restaurant or start the next Starbucks, design the next wrap dress or the next iPod, be a lifesaving nurse, or the scientist who finds a cure for cancer. They may never get there, but however far they go—to the end of their abilities—the path is the path to a flourishing life. "Modern" society still puts roadblock after roadblock in their path. It will take a laser focus for women to reach their ambitions for a full human life. They must even resort to the love that dares not speak its name: love of work.

The world has changed since Friedan wrote, and now mere rhetoric—what we used to call consciousness raising—is not enough. It's a tough world. Women need a plan. Here's mine, for a start.

A Strategic Plan to Get to Work

- Don't study art. Use your education to prepare for a lifetime of work.

- Never quit a job until you have another one. Take work seriously.

- Never know when you're out of milk. Bargain relentlessly for a just household.

- Consider a reproductive strike.

- Get the government you deserve. Stop electing governments that punish women's work. . . .

But as this outline reflects, the changes that will bring women to the positions of power they deserve will come from many places. Change will start when women internalize centuries of hard-won insights into the content of a flourishing life. The next step is for women to stand up for themselves by making and keeping this plan or their own version of it, to lead a flourishing life. Men are not natural villains, but they will not make a fair deal on the home front unless women stand up and ask for one. As the economists say, they never met a man who washed a rented car before he returned it to the lot. It's an old story, but we'll tell it as long as we have to: Only when women make it necessary for men to take on a fair share of the family labor will they do so. . . .

If all of this sounds daunting, it's because for twenty-five years, the only messages women have heard are the ones telling them to forget their dreams and look homeward. For a generation, an acid rain of criticism has fallen daily on the heads of women trying to make a flourishing life in the larger world. No one would want to marry them, the mainstream media said; they were as likely to find a husband as be killed by a terrorist. They'd grow too old to have children, book writers warned them. If they had children, the poor things would be in the hands of "strangers." The only work available involves eighty-hour weeks. Stay-at-home moms suggest that only monsters of neglect would prefer adult work to children's play.

Biases Against Working Mothers

Here's the underlying, unspoken line of thinking that holds women back: Being a mother (but not being a father) is a full-time job. So is being a doctor, lawyer or health executive. No one can successfully do two full-time jobs. A lawyer might be able to juggle many complex cases in various stages of research and negotiation, or a grocery manager might be able to juggle dozens of delivery deadlines and worker schedules, or a doctor might be able to track the data relating to a dozen near-death patients—but a fleeting thought about a daycare drop-off will cause that same woman's on-the-job reliability to evaporate.

"Working mother" is a phrase akin to "deadbeat dad": Both imply someone who is not fulfilling her or his social responsibilities. And so who can be surprised that, according to studies, when men have children, their wages go up—and when women have children, their wages go down? A 2003 Government Accountability Office study found that, among full-time workers, for working fathers, each child increases earnings about 2.1 percent—while for working mothers, each child subtracts 2.5 percent from earnings.

Unexamined stereotypes are like computer viruses: Once they're clicked on—no matter how unintentionally—these unspoken ideas start to dismantle women's careers, which then require a painful amount of time and effort to repair and rebuild. That's mommy tracking in action: Choices are narrowed, and the wage gap is widened. . . .

E.J. Graff, "The Working Mommy Trap,"
TomPaine.com, October 5, 2005.

Once, workingwomen could seek refuge under the umbrella of economic need. But the newest move of the mommy bunch is to contend that mothers should never work unless the alternative is the direst poverty. . . .

The Way We Live Now

The Ultimate Bride, graduate of an Ivy League college and then an English acting school, with a most prestigious master's degree to boot, was the ideal subject for the *New York Times* featured Sunday wedding column "Vows." Walking down the aisle at her family farm, she wed her perfect counterpart, also master's-degree-bearing, and a rising star in the competitive world of global policy.

When she married, the ultimate bride was using her skills and training at a worthy nonprofit. Eight years later, when I tried to interview her for my book on marriage after feminism, I could not find her—or most of the other women who announced their weddings in the *New York Times* that month. He, on the other hand, Googled right up, on the Web site of his current employer, a consulting firm. I called him up.

"Where's your wife?"

"At home in Brooklyn taking care of our daughter."

So were the rest. Eighty-five percent of the thirty-plus January brides in the *New York Times* had left the workplace in whole or in part. All of them were highly educated—degrees in business, including MBAs, lawyers, journalists, an opera singer, doctors, master's of higher education. All of them had worked full time after graduation. Ninety percent of them had had babies since 1996. Half the mothers were not working at all. Roughly one third were in part-time work at varying distances from their education and training. And six of them were working full time.

Although calling women from the 1996 "Styles" section is hardly a scientific survey, the 2002 U.S. Census reports that only 46 percent of the women with graduate degrees and children under one work full time, 17 percent part time. Educated women with children up to eighteen are working 59 percent full time and 18 percent part time, increasing in numbers as the children age. On average, then, highly educated women with small children are working full time at about a fifty percent rate.

Perhaps more important, after three decades of increasing their workforce participation, the percentage of highly educated working mothers has stopped going up. The *New York Times'* part-time home and work columnist, Lisa Belkin, caused a great furor in 2003 when she "sampled" a group of the highly educated stay-at-home mothers she knew and proclaimed there was an "Opt-Out Revolution."

"Revolution" is probably overstating it, but something is clearly going on. In 2001, Harvard Business School professor Myra Hart surveyed the women of the classes of 1981, 1986, and 1991 and found that only 38 percent of female Harvard MBAs with children were working full time. A 2004 survey by the Center for Work-Life Policy of 2,443 women with a graduate degree or very prestigious bachelor's degree revealed that 43 percent of those women with children had taken at least a couple of years out, sometimes more than once, primarily for family reasons. . . .

So what does this "elite minority" have to do with the rest of the world? These educated and privileged women matter. They matter because they are the most likely women to become the rising stars of the new economy—the future senators, deal makers, newspaper editors, research scientists, policy makers, television writers and movie producers, university presidents, and Supreme Court justices. Alarm bells should ring when people say things like elites don't matter only when the subject is women. You never see the *New York Times*, or for that matter the lefty *Nation* magazine, arguing that Congress's decisions don't matter, because most people aren't congressmen. Can you imagine the *Wall Street Journal* asserting that CEOs' decisions don't matter because most people can't aspire to be CEOs? Ever read in the sports page that quarterbacks don't matter because they are the elite of football teams? Or that Henry Ford IV doesn't matter because most auto workers are not presidents of Ford?

Why would leading *women* matter? Well, media surveys reveal, for instance, that if only one member of a television show's creative staff is female, the percentage of women on-screen goes up from 36 percent to 42 percent. A world of 84 percent male lawyers and 84 percent female assistants is a different place from one with women role models in positions of social authority. Think of a big American city with an 84 percent white police force. If role models don't matter, consider how an all-male Supreme Court is going to feel. We are about to find out, I fear. Highly educated women's abandonment of the workplace is not an extension of the centuries of upper-class arm candy; it's a sex-specific brain drain from the future rulers of our society.

But interestingly these select women are not alone. Without regard to class, in 2004, only 38 percent of married mothers with husbands and children under one in the house worked full time—13 percent work part time, another 3 percent are looking for work. Married women with children under five and a husband around worked at a rate of only 62 percent, but, again, about one third of that statistic is probably women doing part-time work. Whether the trend is for increasing participation or not, the raw numbers are low. Moreover, the assignment of responsibility for the household to women applies in every social class. . . .

Choosing Your Choice

The most disheartening part about women's deciding to stay home is that they say doing so is their choice. "Choice" is the weasel word, and it is legitimated, especially for women who consider themselves liberals, because it's been adopted by the feminist movement. Even the most empowered women do not see how narrow their options are at the moment of "choice." . . .

The leveling off of women's professional ambitions today shows us one truth: Without a movement to support them, women are not choosing the path to status and power alone. My little survey of the brides of the *Times* reflects that feminism lost even the women who had the most opportunity to *choose* the path toward status and power—the geeky and quirky intellectuals, not the prom queens and debutantes. Take a look at any Sunday *Times*. Although most of the brides have the bloom of youth, the wedding portion of the "Styles" section no longer resembles a debutante party. Just to cite a random example, on Sunday, January 15, 2006, the featured "Vows" bride, a Ph.D. from Cambridge University, was the curator of manuscripts at the Folger Shakespeare Library in Washington. Other brides included a medical student who was magna cum laude at Harvard; a Harvard Law grad associate at Arnold & Porter; an ob-gyn, cum laude from Columbia; deputy director in the Mayor's Office of Special Projects and Community Events in New York with a master's degree in public administration from Columbia; and so on. . . .

These were the girls who were going to make their lives from their wits and their brains, not their looks, trust funds, and reproductive organs. Immensely desirable mates, they should have been able to find spouses whose needs would not require, overtly or covertly, that they quit their jobs. Gifted with capacities for refined scholarship, human healing, legal reasoning, and educated to use the capacities, they were the women for whom the constraints of the feminine mystique were the most unjust. The twentieth-century feminist movement was the beginning, opening up the public world of work to women but leaving the family untouched. The Opt-Out Revolution may be in reality only a leveling off, but in this context it is the end of the beginning.

Deafened by choice, here's the moral analysis these women never heard: The family—with its repetitious, socially invisible, physical tasks—is a necessary part of life and has obvious emotional and immediate rewards, but it allows fewer opportunities for full human flourishing than public spheres like the market or the government. This less flourishing sphere is not the natural or moral responsibility only of women. Therefore, assigning it to women is unjust. Women assigning it to themselves is equally unjust.

The choice is a false one, based on the realities of a half-revolutionized society. Once we recognize that, we can admit that the tools feminism offered women to escape the dilemma have failed. . . .

| "We can afford to take time out of our
forty-year careers to raise our children."

Mothers Should Stay at Home

Suzanne Venker

Suzanne Venker is a former middle-school English teacher, a writer, and a full-time mother. In the following viewpoint she argues that mothers should stay home with their children because it is worthwhile to mothers and children. She asserts that women are led to believe the careers are necessary for happiness when in reality the joys of homemaking and childrearing are far more fulfilling. She counters claims that it is not economically feasible for mothers not to work by recommending that women plan for having children and that they take the job seriously.

As you read, consider the following questions:

1. According to the author, how has motherhood changed since the 1950s?

2. In 1999, how much money was made from the sale of self-help books?

3. According to the author, what is one of the results of women not planning ahead for motherhood?

It's a cultural shift that's been long in coming. "For the first time in 25 years, the proportion of working mothers with children under one year old posted a decline, to 55% in 2000 from 59% in 1998," writes [cultural researcher] Sue Shellenbarger. There are several reasons for this turnaround. For one thing, the Generation x'ers have witnessed the Baby Boomers' attempt to have it all and do not want that life for themselves. "Many young women express surprising ambivalence about their working mothers' lives and are attracted to a different goal: to be with their children as they grow and not rely on babysitters, as their mothers did," writes Marie Brenner, author of *Great Dames: What I Learned from Older Women*. Women have also discovered that the workplace isn't all it's cracked up to be. "I think women are beginning to feel betrayed by work. What they see at work, this identity, community, meaning, is not being found" says work historian Benjamin Hunnicutt. Women have to come to realize that it makes no sense to have children if one's intention is to find them another home in which to spend the majority of their waking hours. A former working mother, Margaret Cox observes, "Before I knew I was expecting my third child, I had a kind of epiphany. Although I loved my job and had a great one, I needed to be at home for my boys. I knew I had to make a difference in their lives. I needed to raise them myself." Finally, many women now accept that they do not really "have to work"—despite rampant use of this rationalization—because they recognize that having to do without some things is not the same as being poor.

Thankfully, motherhood no longer means living a life akin to that of the 1950s housewife. Not only have house dresses been replaced with work-out garb, mothers have every convenience they could ask for: dishwashers, disposable diapers, washing machines, microwaves, VCRs, cordless and hands-free phones, computers, and the Internet. The days of traditional homemaking are long gone. Women can now spend the bulk of their time enjoying their children. More important, though, women now accept that the issue of combining work and motherhood has little to do with gender (that is, a woman's "place") and everything to do with practicality and feasibility. They are also discovering, much to their surprise, that they actually like being with their children. Who would have thought that despite the hard work and sacrifice, small, little beings could bring such pleasure and satisfaction? Appears society has kept such details hidden away.

Simply put, more and more women now recognize the enormous value—indeed, the basic necessity—of a house being a home, rather than a place to sleep and shower. They are content with the vast options women have today and place the most value on one of these: motherhood. To them, it is a profession and a privilege, not a jail sentence. Although their careers are on hold, they are multifaceted women, not beholden to a job for their happiness or self-esteem. They are certain their lives are meant for more than receiving a paycheck and that the moments of childhood come only once in a lifetime. "We want, at the end of our lives, to look back and see that what we have done amounts to more than a pile of pay stubs, that we have loved and been loved." writes [Canadian author] Danielle Crittenden.

Unhappy in the Workplace

Unfortunately, many women still haven't made the connection between their choice to have it all and their overall sense of despondency. In 1999, $500 million dollars worth of self-help books were sold. *Five hundred million dollars.* It seems to me that if what Betty Friedan said [in 1963's bestseller *The Feminine Mystique*] were true—that raising children is a life of "empty, purposeless days" and that self-fulfillment is the only path to a woman's true identity—women would be too busy being happy and fulfilled to scour the self-help section of their local bookstore. "I don't think women as a group are much happier now than they were in the 50s" says psychologist Mary Pipher. Indeed they are not, and the reason for this is that Friedan's solution to the "problem that has no name" was bogus. It is good for women to be recognized for their many capabilities outside of motherhood; but the fact remains that most women do not find happiness by pursuing careers at the expense of motherhood.

Many people to whom women have turned have told them, in no uncertain terms, that it is impossible to have it all. Dr. Phil, known best for his ability to "tell it like it is" tells readers in the September 2001 edition of *O* magazine, "Life is about tough choices. I have never encountered a successful person who didn't have to sacrifice in one area of her life to be more successful in another. If you put more into your career, kids and family suffer; if you put more into family, career suffers. That's the bottom line." Financial guru Suze Orman tells us that financial freedom can only be achieved by giving up certain things we want. Oprah tells us that it is through giving to others that we grow as human beings: "When you shift your focus from success to service, your work will instantly have more meaning." The Dalai Lama tells us that material possessions mean nothing in the end and that true fulfillment can only be gained through sacrifice. And Gary Zukav explains that one's soul can never be at peace if we are always looking for more. In *Seat of the Soul*, he writes, "If you follow your feelings, you become aware of the different parts of yourself, and the different things they want. You cannot have all of them at once because many of them conflict. The fulfillment of one part of you creates anguish in another, or others, and you are torn." It is this feeling of being torn between career and motherhood that leaves women feeling empty. Women just don't realize that grass always looks greener on the other side—but rarely is.

Career and motherhood are not equal and interchangeable. Many women have failed to find a sense of purpose in

Planning Ahead to Stay at Home

Living on one income is not as difficult as some people think, says Mark Oleson, director of the Financial Counseling Clinic at Iowa State University. He encourages couples to practice living on one income to prove that it's possible.

"If you think of it in terms of lower taxes, and the fact that you might not need a second car and that you won't have child-care expenses, you could discover that it's more realistic than you imagined," says Oleson.

Too often, people convince themselves that they can't make it without ever sitting down and taking a hard look at the possibilities.

Athens, Ohio, mom Tori Griffith and her husband did exactly that. After rolling back her work hours in her human resources job to part-time, she still felt that she was spread too thin between her office and her home. She and her husband began to prepare.

"The best thing we were able to do was to begin paying off our debts," she says. "We practiced living on one salary and put all of the other toward debt."

They also got in the habit of paying ahead on the principal of their mortgage and cutting back on personal spending habits. Other couples have used the same theory and put one spouse's salary toward needs for the baby until its arrival, buying a crib one month, a car seat the next, and so on, rather than racking up a heap of credit card debt right before the birth.

Tracy Zollinger Turner, "Plan to Stay at Home with the Kids,"
Bankrate.com, 2007.

the workforce, but few women fail to find a sense of purpose at home. As Orenstein writes about the women she interviewed for her book, "Questions of career and achievement just didn't drive women the way they once had. The voice of ambition I'd heard in women had modulated from eager to conflicted to disinterested." One woman tells her, "By your mid-forties you're supposed to have attained a certain level professionally, and most of us actually have. But it's just . . . so what? What are you going to do? Buy more things? Make more money?" And yet, if you asked another group of women who had spent the same amount of time pursuing full-time motherhood, few—if any—would feel that their children didn't "drive them the way they once had" or that their feelings about motherhood "had modulated from eager to conflicted to disinterested." And that's because there is no comparison between one's children and one's career. Raising children will always be more satisfying and valuable than any other work we do.

In the end, many women have come to learn that the only road to happiness is a sense of place and that this sense of place cannot be found at work. [Songwriter and Iternet activist] John Perry Barlow defines happiness this way: "Happiness is not a solitary endeavor; it's a joint enterprise, something that can only be created by the whole. Contentment arises from a sense of family, community, and connectedness. Such virtues are in dwindling supply in America." And the reason they are dwindling is that working motherhood pulls women further and away from this goal. The faster we move and the more we do, the less time we have for family. Moreover, says Barlow, sacrifice has been underrated: "We have come to regard service as a self-suppressing obligation rather than a self-fulfilling responsibility. It doesn't have to be that way."

Planning for Motherhood

Unfortunately, many women have yet to accept this fact. Consequently, they do not take the time to consider why they want children in the first place or what the purpose of motherhood is. Not only do they not think about the emotional and financial aspects of motherhood, they do not ask themselves if they are ready for a career change that will require them to make huge sacrifices. Women ignore these issues and go into motherhood blindly, irresponsibly. Part of the reason they can do this is that society doesn't encourage women to plan for motherhood. Women are not expected to curtail their lives to suit the needs of children—so what's to think about? According to modern-day society, motherhood only requires women to make it through pregnancy and childbirth (Have you seen the array of books on this subject?), find a "quality" caregiver, and resume life as normal. As a result, the average woman today [as of 2004] gives very little thought to the realities of motherhood until the day her baby arrives. As [columnist Meghan Cox] Gurdon observes, "I discovered how tricky it can be for thirty-something professionals like me to immerse ourselves in domesticity when our lifelong expectations, and virtually all of our role models, are outside of it."

One of the results of women not planning ahead for motherhood is that they presume their circumstances to be a matter of luck. Women are lucky to be able to conceive. They are lucky if they are able to stay home with their children. They are lucky if they have their mothers nearby. They are lucky if they have the kind of job that allows them to work from home. They are lucky if their husbands pull their weight at home. Amidst all these fortunate circumstances, it's hard to believe that there are any happy full-time mothers. But there are. For what many women don't consider is the fact that some women plan their lives around motherhood, rather than planning motherhood around their lives. Some women create a life for themselves that is conducive to raising children. "If there's a single, remarkable generational difference between the Boomers and the Gen-xers, it's that more of the younger women are now planning at this stage of their lives," writes [freelance journalist] Susan Brenna.

And so can you.

Planning for motherhood requires women to start thinking about children soon after they graduate from college, the idea being that if they give motherhood at least as much attention as they do their careers—if not more—they can then strike that balance they are so desperately seeking. They can plan to have children and a career—but separately. Or they can plan to incorporate some type of work with motherhood in a way that will not interfere with their obligation to their children. Thinking about children at the age of twenty-two does not mean women need to get married. On the contrary, I think most people should wait to settle down. It does mean that they must begin thinking about their desire to raise children and the need to be out of the workforce for a short time. Maybe not for eighteen years—though this should certainly be an option—but for five or six at least. . . .

Paradigm Shift

It's time to shift our paradigm. Women must begin to view motherhood as something they get to do rather than something they have to squeeze into their hectic career lives. Motherhood is a career, not a sideline occupation. As one woman tells [sociologist] Peggy Orenstein, "The kids are now my work. They are my job. And in the same way that I was a perfectionist at work and cared a great deal about the product and about winning and all of those things, that has been translated over to my kids." Furthermore, women have plenty of time to pursue their own interests. Not only do we have time to focus on ourselves before we have children, we have the rest of our lives—after our children are grown—to become self-absorbed again. "Just as the young never really understand, or believe, that there is a long, long time stretching ahead of them in which to do all the things they want, so many young mothers continue to feel that if they don't move on the question of career now, the world will simply pass them by," writes [journalist] Midge Decter. It makes little sense to eschew the power and flexibility that comes from raising children solely because we fear who we might become without our jobs. There is no reason to try to do everything at once. We can afford to take time out of our forty-year careers to raise our children. Yes, putting one's career on the back burner may put some of us at a disadvantage when we enter the workforce again, but not doing so will put us at a disadvantage with our children—and our souls. Motherhood changes who we are. It is a gift, a chance to become a better person. What could be more liberating than that?

Contrary to what the women's movement would have us believe, the traditional family structure is not something that holds women down. The traditional family structure simply keeps women from having to worry about producing an income while they work on the most important job of their lives. And most husbands—even if they keep it to themselves—want to support them. One of the main reasons my generation has not been successful with marriage and family is that we do not view the family as a permanent unit, with two people working toward the same goal. Today's women are taught to be responsible for themselves, first and foremost, so that in case their marriages dissolve, they will have well-paying jobs. But this philosophy has failed. . . .

It is abundantly clear that the philosophy of the last several decade—this Everyone for Himself philosophy—has failed. As the current divorce rate shows, there is no longer any incentive to settle down. This is why it is imperative that we re-evaluate the purpose of the traditional family, with one parent at home and one parent in the workforce. Until we do, Americans will never again be successful in raising strong families. It seems to me that the secret to making sense of career and motherhood is to see beyond the here and now, beyond our immediate wants and desires. If I had given up and gone back to work when my daughter was in her first year of life, merely because the transition was so jarring and her crying incessant, I would never have known the joy and sense of fulfillment I know now. It is because I stuck it out, waited patiently (a trait I needed to learn anyway), and worked hard every day to develop a relationship with my daughter that we share a strong bond. Does this mean she will always be the perfect child or that I will never struggle as a parent simply because I stayed home with her? Of course not. But it does mean that she knows I will be here for her tomorrow. And the next day. And the day after that. It means that she can count on me, not to be a perfect mother, but a stable force in her life. Most important, it means that she knows I consider her worth my time and attention.

And this will mark her soul for a lifetime.

> "The struggle for equal marriage rights
> is a feminist issue, because women will
> not be equal until they can pursue their
> dreams free from discrimination."

Women Should Support Same-Sex Marriage

National Organization for Women

The National Organization for Women (NOW) was founded in 1966 to fight for the equality of all women and is the largest feminist activist organization in the United States. In the following viewpoint NOW argues that feminists should support the legalization of same-sex marriage. They assert that until lesbians and gays are granted the right to marry, women will continue to lack equality. Making same-sex marriage legal will extend the same rights to lesbians and gays that are given to heterosexuals.

As you read, consider the following questions:

1. In what year did NOW issue its first policy statement recognizing lesbian rights as a feminist issue?
2. When was the Defense of Marriage Act passed?
3. According to the authors, about how many federal protections and rights are same-sex couples denied?

National Organization for Women, "Same-Sex Marriage Is a Feminist Issue," *www .now.org*, May 17, 2004. Copyright © 1995–2007. All rights reserved. Reproduced by permission.

In the battle for lesbian and gay rights, the issue of equal marriage rights has taken center stage. In a crucial election year, and with many other issues on the table affecting women, why are feminists advocating for same-sex marriage rights?

NOW's History on Lesbian Rights

[National Organization of Women] NOW's mission is to promote equality for women—all women. The human and civil rights of all women are included in this effort. For more than 30 years, NOW has been a leader in the struggle for lesbian rights. In 1971 NOW issued its first policy statement recognizing lesbian rights as a feminist issue. The statement acknowledged that a woman's right to independence and self-determination includes the right to define and express her own sexuality and to choose her own lifestyle. This policy cited some of the more blatant forms of discrimination against lesbians—employment, education, child custody and marriage—emphasizing that lesbian couples are denied all the economic and legal benefits granted to married women, including tax deductions, insurance benefits, inheritance rights and more.

Throughout the next three decades, NOW's work on lesbian rights remained strong and decisive, covering such issues as discrimination in the military, anti-sodomy laws, electing lesbian and gay candidates to political office, hate crimes legislation, and expanding same-sex partners' rights. In 1995, NOW made official its support for same-sex marriage, stating that the choice of marriage is a fundamental constitutional right, protected under the equal protection clause of the Fourteenth Amendment, and should not be denied because of a person's sexual orientation.

NOW continues to advocate for lesbian rights, including the right to share fully and equally in the rights and responsibilities of marriage. . . .

Same-Sex Marriage Emerges
as a Dominant Issue

For years, the Lesbian/Gay/Bisexual/Transgender and feminist communities have recognized that same-sex couples cannot participate fully in our society if they are denied the rights and responsibilities offered to heterosexual couples through marriage. This has led to cases in various states where same-sex couples have filed suit in order to secure their right to marry, and NOW has participated in amicus curiae (or "friend of the court") briefs in those cases.

The right wing immediately seized upon this issue to rally its ultra-conservative supporters. Like the issues of reproductive rights and affirmative action, same-sex marriage can be used to stir up feelings of fear, intolerance and hate. It is also used as a wedge issue, in order to split apart groups that might otherwise agree on issues and pit them against each other.

The Defense of Marriage Act (DOMA), passed in 1996 and signed by former President Bill Clinton, defined marriage as "the legal union between one man and one woman," and asserted that no state is required to recognize a same-sex marriage performed in another state. In addition, 38 states have passed their own Defense of Marriage acts.

In 2000, then-governor Howard Dean signed a law granting civil unions to same-sex couples in Vermont, making it the most comparable option to marriage in the country. Both California and Hawaii have passed domestic partnership laws, which offer same-sex couples some of the benefits given to married people, but fall far short of providing equal treatment. None of these options offer the hundreds of federal benefits available to married couples.

On Nov. 18, 2003, the Massachusetts Supreme Court made history by ruling that both same-sex and opposite-sex couples are entitled to equal marriage rights under the Massachusetts State Constitution. On Feb. 4, 2004, the same court clarified its ruling, stating that only access to civil marriage (not civil unions) would provide equal protection to same-sex couples under the state constitution.

Terrified that the fight will come next to the U.S. Supreme Court, and that a slim majority of justices might find laws denying equal marriage rights unconstitutional, the radical right is attempting to amend the U.S. Constitution. The Federal Marriage Amendment, introduced in the House of Representatives and the Senate, and supported by President George W. Bush, is an attempt to write discrimination and bigotry into our Constitution, and to overrule any state action on behalf of equal marriage rights.

Why Not Civil Unions or Partnerships?

While the practice of granting civil unions or partnerships to same-sex couples at the state level has been an important advance in the fight for equality, these options do not carry the full legal benefits or the cultural significance of marriage. The substitution of civil unions, in fact, assigns same-sex couples to second-class status—separate and unequal.

Same-sex couples across the country are denied more than 1,000 federal protections and rights. Most states deny committed lesbian and gay couples hundreds of additional benefits. These federal and state rights range from the ability to file joint tax returns to the crucial responsibility of making decisions on a partner's behalf in a medical emergency.

The inability to marry has both emotional and financial consequences. Same-sex couples are not allowed to share Social Security, Medicare, Family and Medical Leave, health care, disability, military and other benefits. They cannot inherit 401(k)s and other property from their life partner without a will. According to Lambda Legal, same-sex couples can lose more than $10,000 per year upon retirement due to a lack of Social Security benefits that would be bestowed upon opposite-sex married couples in identical situations.

Federal Protections and Rights Denied Gay and Lesbian Couples

According to a 1997 report released by the General Accounting Office, gays and lesbian couples are denied more than 1,400 federal protections and benefits. They are denied these rights even in states where gay marriage is legal because the Defense of Marriage Act states that the federal government only recognizes marriage as "a legal union of one man and one woman as husband and wife".

Here are some of the legal rights that married couples have and gays and lesbians are denied:

- Joint parental rights of children
- Joint adoption
- Status as "next-of-kin" for hospital visits and medical decisions
- Domestic violence protection orders
- Spousal veterans benefits
- Social Security
- Medicare
- Wrongful death benefits for surviving partner and children
- Bereavement or sick leave to care for partner or children
- Child support
- Joint insurance plans
- Welfare and public assistance
- Joint housing for elderly
- Credit protection

Kathy Belge, "What are the Legal Benefits of Marriage?"
http://lesbianlife.about.com, 2007.

This discrimination also affects the children of same-sex couples. Lesbian and gay parents are unable to assume parenting rights and responsibilities when children are brought into a family through birth, adoption, surrogacy or other means. In most states, there is no law guaranteeing a non-custodial, biological or adoptive parent's visitation rights or requiring child support from such a parent.

With an argument this strong on behalf of equal marriage rights, the right wing has had to resort to absurd claims. The charge, repeated over and over again, that allowing lesbian and gay couples to wed will somehow tarnish the institution of marriage makes little sense. When many people hear the phrase "the institution of marriage" they think of unions sanctified by the church. However, the struggle for same-sex marriage is about legal rights—it does not demand that churches perform same-sex marriage ceremonies.

This right-wing propaganda also ignores the fact that many same-sex couples, a large number of them with children, already exist, and will continue to exist regardless of a constitutional amendment. Won't giving these families the rights and benefits they deserve make them stronger? And if more families are flourishing, isn't that good for marriage in general and our society as a whole?

The struggle for equal marriage rights is a feminist issue, because women will not be equal until they can pursue their dreams free from discrimination.

> "Gay marriage takes something that belongs essentially to women, is crucial to their very freedom, and empties it of meaning."

Women Should Not Support Same-Sex Marriage

Sam Schulman

Sam Schulman is a freelance writer who focuses on politics and morals. In the following viewpoint he argues that legalizing same-sex marriage will hurt women. He asserts that the point of marriage is to bring together opposites—a man and a woman— for the good of reproducing and caring for offspring, which is not possible for same-sex couples. Also, he notes that marriage is important in regulating female sexuality.

As you read, consider the following questions:

1. What are the origins of the word "marriage"?
2. According to the author, what is the fundamental advantage of marriage for women?
3. According to the author, what are the two most important achievements of the women's movement of the late 1960s?

Sam Schulman, "Gay Marriage—and Marriage," *Commentary*, vol. 116, November 2003. Copyright © 2003 by the American Jewish Committee. All rights reserved. Reproduced by permission of the publisher and the author.-

The feeling seems to be growing that gay marriage is inevitably coming our way in the U.S., perhaps through a combination of judicial fiat and legislation in individual states. Growing, too, is the sense of a shift in the climate of opinion. The American public seems to be in the process of changing its mind—not actually in favor of gay marriage, but toward a position of slightly revolted tolerance for the idea: Survey results suggest that people have forgotten why they were so opposed to the notion even as recently as a few years ago.

It is curious that this has happened so quickly. With honorable exceptions, most of those who are passionately on the side of the traditional understanding of marriage appear to be at a loss for words to justify their passion; as for the rest, many seem to wish gay marriage had never been proposed in the first place, but also to have resigned themselves to whatever happens. In this respect, the gay-marriage debate is very different from the abortion debate, in which few with an opinion on either side have been so disengaged.

I think I understand why this is the case: as someone passionately and instinctively opposed to the idea of homosexual marriage, I have found myself disappointed by the arguments I have seen advanced against it. The strongest of these arguments predict measurable harm to the family and to our arrangements for the upbringing and well-being of children. I do not doubt the accuracy of those arguments. But they do not seem to get at the heart of the matter. . . .

The Purpose of Marriage

The truth is banal, circular, but finally unavoidable: by definition, the essence of marriage is to sanction and solemnize that connection of opposites which alone creates new life. (Whether or not a given married couple does in fact create new life is immaterial.) Men and women can marry only because they belong to different, opposite, sexes. In marriage, they surrender those separate and different sexual allegiances, coming together to form a new entity. Their union is not a formalizing of romantic love but represents a certain idea—a construction, an abstract thought—about how best to formalize the human condition. This thought, embodied in a promise or a contract, is what holds marriage together, and the creation of this idea of marriage marks a key moment in the history of human development, a triumph over the alternative idea, which is concubinage.

Let me try to be more precise. Marriage can only concern my connection to a woman (and not to a man) because, as my reference to concubinage suggests, marriage is an institution that is built around female sexuality and female procreativity. (The very word "marriage" comes from the Latin word for mother, mater.) It exists for the gathering-in of a woman's sexuality under the protective net of the human or divine order, or both. This was so in the past and it is so even now, in our supposedly liberated times, when a woman who is in a sexual relationship without being married is, and is perceived to be, in a different state of being (not just a different legal state) from a woman who is married.

Marriage and Sex

Circumstances have, admittedly, changed. Thanks to contraception, the decision to marry no longer precedes sexual intercourse as commonly as it did 50 years ago, when, for most people, a fully sexual relationship could begin only with marriage (and, when, as my mother constantly reminds me, one married for sex). Now the decision can come later, but come it almost certainly must. Even with contraception, even with feminism and women's liberation, the feeling would appear to be nearly as strong as ever that, for a woman, a sexual relationship must either end in marriage, or end.

This is surely understandable, for marriage benefits women, again not just in law but essentially. A woman can control who is the father of her children only insofar as there

Gay Marriage Hurts Heterosexual Marriages

So, exactly how does legalizing same-sex marriage hurt our marriages, our children and our society?

Once we abandon marriage to the whims and desires of adults seeking validation of their sexual lifestyles, we denigrate children and their needs—legally validating relationships that would deliberately leave them motherless or fatherless. And that hurts society. We have plenty of data to show what happens to children when they grow up without a father or a mother. Prisons are filled with adults who were fatherless as children. The financial burden of welfare and prison programs on society as a result of children growing up without their mother or their father is horrific. And that is not even taking into consideration the immense personal suffering that inevitably is too often hidden behind these statistics. . . .

If you change the definition of marriage you sever it from its very purpose for existing—you sever reproduction from parenthood and that is a radical experiment. If you say gender doesn't matter to marriage, then you are also saying that gender doesn't matter to parenthood. . . .

The institution of marriage discriminates to make sure that those who marry have the potential to create children in order to perpetuate the human race and that the union will provide children with what they need most—a mother and a father legally bound together in a family relationship. Marriage confers benefits to potential parents as they create and rear children. The government does not care whom you love. The government has no interest in sanctioning love, friendship, or personal associations. It has a vital interest in encouraging what is best for society.

Sharon Slater, "How Does Legalizing Same-Sex Marriage Hurt Marriage, Children and Society?" Meridian Magazine, 2004.

is a civil and private order that protects her from rape; marriage is the bulwark of that order. The 1960's feminists had the right idea: the essential thing for a woman is to control her own body. But they were wrong that this is what abortion is for; it is, rather, what marriage is for. It is humanity's way of enabling a woman to control her own body and to know (if she cares to) who is the father of her children.

Yes, marriage tends to regulate or channel the sexual appetite of men, and this is undoubtedly a good thing for women. But it is not the ultimate good. A husband, no matter how unfaithful, cannot introduce a child who is not his wife's own into a marriage without her knowledge; she alone has the power to do such a thing. For a woman, the fundamental advantage of marriage is thus not to regulate her husband but to empower herself—to regulate who has access to her person, and to marshal the resources of her husband and of the wider community to help her raise her children.

Every human relationship can be described as an enslavement, but for women the alternative to marriage is a much worse enslavement—which is why marriage, for women, is often associated as much with sexual freedom as with sexual constraint. In the traditional Roman Catholic cultures of the Mediterranean and South America, where virginity is fiercely protected and adolescent girls are hardly permitted to "date," marriage gives a woman the double luxury of controlling her sexuality and, if she wishes, extending it.

For men, by contrast, the same phenomenon—needing to be married in order to feel safe and free in a sexual relationship—simply does not exist. Men may wish to marry, but for more particular reasons: because they want to have children, or because they want to make a woman they love happy, or because they fear they will otherwise lose the woman they love. But it is rare for a man to feel essentially incomplete, or unprotected, in a sexual relationship that has not been solem nized by marriage. In fact, a man desperate to marry is often considered to have something wrong with him—to be unusually controlling or needy.

Impact on Children

Because marriage is an arrangement built around female sexuality, because the institution has to do with women far more than it has to do with men, women will be the victims of its destruction. Those analysts who have focused on how children will suffer from the legalization of gay marriage are undoubtedly correct—but this will not be the first time that social developments perceived as advances for one group or another have harmed children. After all, the two most important (if effortless) achievements of the women's movement of the late 1960's were the right to abort and the right—in some social classes, the commandment—to join the professional workforce, both manifestly harmful to the interests of children.

But with the success of the gay-liberation movement, it is women themselves, all women, who will be hurt. The reason is that gay marriage takes something that belongs essentially to women, is crucial to their very freedom, and empties it of meaning.

Periodical Bibliography

The following articles have been selected to supplement the diverse views presented in this chapter.

Gloria Borger	"The Mommy Factor," *U.S. News & World Report*, February 12, 2007.
Rachel Bowlby	"Generations," *Textual Practice*, March 2007.
Lianne George and Barbara Righton	"State of Our Unions," *Maclean's*, February 19, 2007.
Michele Hoffnung	"What's in a Name? Marital Name Choice Revisited," *Sex Roles*, December 2006.
Gayle Kaufman and Frances Goldscheider	"Do Men 'Need' a Spouse More than Women?" *Sociological Quarterly*, February 2007.
Julia Krane and Linda Davies	"Mothering Under Difficult Circumstances," *Affilia: Women & Social Work*, Spring 2007.
Bonnie Mann	"Gay Marriage and the War on Terror," *Hypatia*, Winter 2007.
Clelia Mannino and Francine Deutsch	"Changing the Division of Household Labor: A Negotiated Process Between Partners," *Sex Roles*, March 2007.
Meave O'Brien	"Mothers' Emotional Care Work in Education and Its Moral Imperative," *Gender & Education*, March 2007.
Stephanie Rosenbloom	"Evolution of a Feminist Daughter," *New York Times*, March 18, 2007.
Maria João Silveirinha	"Displacing the 'Political,'" *Feminist Media Studies*, March 2007.
Wendy Somerson	"Knot in Our Name," *Bitch Magazine: Feminist Response to Pop Culture*, Winter 2007.
W. Bradford Wilcox and Steven L. Nock	"'Her' Marriage after the Revolutions," *Sociological Forum*, March 2007.

For Further Discussion

Chapter 1

1. The diversity of viewpoints in this chapter demonstrates the difficulty in defining feminism as Sally Haslanger and Nancy Tuana argue. How have these viewpoints shaped your definition of feminism as a concept and as a movement?

2. Kay S. Hymowitz argues that feminism is obsolete, while Jade Maestre argues that there is still much for the movement to accomplish. Whose viewpoint do you find most convincing, and why?

3. What evidence does Phyllis Chesler offer to support her view for why Western feminists should fight for the rights of Islamic women? How does Susan Muaddi Darraj describe the misconceptions American women hold about Middle Eastern women and feminism? How does each viewpoint influence your understanding of the issue?

Chapter 2

1. Stephanie Cleveland argues that pornography is harmful to women. Barbara Dority argues that pornography can be liberating for women. After reading these two viewpoints, what effect do you think pornography has on women? Explain your view.

2. Kimberly Klinger argues that women should have the right to be prostitutes, while the Coalition Against Trafficking in Women—Asia Pacific argues that they do not. Which viewpoint offers the strongest evidence? Explain your answer.

3. Ellie Levenson and Alex Mason debate the safety and morality of the morning-after pill. Which viewpoint is more convincing? Why?

4. The Center for Reproductive Rights uses statistics and other data to argue that women have the right to safe and legal abortions. Frederica Mathewes-Green uses personal experience to argue that women do not have the right to abortions. Which type of evidence is more persuasive? Why?

Chapter 3

1. Arrah Nielsen argues that women do not make less money than men because of discrimination in the workplace, but because they choose to accept lower paying jobs and to work less hours. Stephanie Seguino argues that women may earn less than men because of societal expectations about gender. Based on these viewpoints, why do you think women make less than men? Explain your answer.

2. A writer for the *Economist* argues that the glass ceiling still exists for women in the workplace, while Lindsay McNutt argues that it never existed in the first place. Based on the evidence offered, do you think women are held back from the highest corporate positions because of the glass ceiling? Why or why not?

3. Tony Campolo argues that women should be allowed to serve as church leaders, while Wayne Grudem believes that it would be against Christian teachings for women to preach from the pulpit. Which viewpoint is more persuasive? Explain your answer.

4. What evidence does Robin Gerber use to argue that women should serve in military combat? What evidence does Mackubin Thomas Owens use to argue that women should not serve in military combat? Whose viewpoint is most convincing to you, and why?

Chapter 4

1. Lynn Marcotte explains that feminists can be pro-family, while Andreas J. Köstenberger argues that feminism has destroyed the American family. How does Lynn Marcotte argue her case? How does each viewpoint impact your opinion of the relationship between feminism and family values? Explain your answer.

2. What evidence does Linda Hirshman offer for why mothers should work? What evidence does Suzanne Venker offer for why mothers should stay at home? Whose viewpoint is most convincing? Why?

3. The National Organization for Women argues that feminists should support gay marriage initiatives. Sam Schulman argues that gay marriage hurts women. What role should feminists play in the gay marriage debate? Explain your answer.

Organizations to Contact

The editors have compiled the following list of organizations concerned with the issues debated in this book. The descriptions are derived from materials provided by the organizations. All have publications or information available for interested readers. The list was compiled on the date of publication of the present volume; the information provided here may change. Be aware that many organizations take several weeks or longer to respond to inquiries, so allow as much time as possible.

Association for Women in Psychology (AWP)
Department of Counseling, Indiana State University
Terre Haute, IN 47809
(812) 237-7693
e-mail: mcboyer@indstate.edu
Web site: www.awpsych.org

Founded in 1969, AWP is a not-for-profit scientific and educational organization committed to encouraging feminist psychological research, theory, and activism. AWP frequently collaborates with other organizations in promoting a feminist approach to research, teaching, and mental health and has been an official Non-Governmental Organization of the United Nations since 1976. In addition to annual national and international conferences, the AWP regularly publishes a newsletter and books that focus on feminist issues in psychology, including *Bias in Psychiatric Diagnosis*.

Association of Libertarian Feminists (ALF)
484 Lake Park Ave., #24, Oakland, CA 94610-2730
Web site: www.alf.org

Founded in 1973, ALF encourages women to become economically self-sufficient and psychologically independent; publicizes and promotes realistic attitudes toward female competence, achievement, and potential; opposes the abridgement of individual rights by any government on account of sex; and works toward changing sexist attitudes and behavior exhibited by individuals. In addition to a regular newsletter, ALF regularly publishes articles and discussion papers that focus on the equality of women. Titles include "The Right to Abortion: A Libertarian Defense" and "Government Is Women's Enemy."

Center for the Advancement of Women (CAW)

25 West 43rd Street, Ste. 1120, New York, NY   10036
(212) 391-7718 • fax: (212) 391-7720
e-mail: info@advancewomen.org
Web site: www.advancewomen.org

The CAW is a not-for-profit, independent, nonpartisan research and public education institution established to advance women's equal participation at every level of society. The CAW, which was formerly known as the Center for Gender Equality, regularly sponsors research focusing on the status of women. Its research reports include *Progress and Perils: How Gender Issues Unite and Divide Women*, *The Impact of Terrorist Attacks on Women*, and *Women Are Becoming Both More Religious & More Conservative*.

Feminist Majority Foundation (FMF)

1600 Wilson Boulevard, Ste. 801, Arlington, VA   22209
(703) 522-2214 • fax: (703) 522-2219
Web site: http://feminist.org

FMF is dedicated to women's equality, improved reproductive health, and promotion of non-violence. Since 1987 FMF has engaged in research and public policy development, public education programs, grassroots organizing projects, leadership training and development programs, and it participates in and organizes forums on issues of women's equality and empowerment. In addition to regular reports and resources for teachers, FMF also publishes books such as *The Feminist Chronicles* and a regular newsletter, *Feminist Majority Report*.

Feminists for Free Expression (FFE)
e-mail: freedom@well.com
Web site: www.ffeusa.org

FFE is a non-profit organization that provides a leading voice opposing state and national legislation that threatens free speech; defends the right to free expression in court cases, including those before the Supreme Court; supports the rights of artists whose works have been suppressed or censored and provides expert speakers to universities, law schools, and the media throughout the country. Founded in 1992, FFE believes freedom of expression is especially important for women's rights. In addition to a regular newsletter, FFE has published The Free Speech Pamphlet Series, which focused on such issues as the Internet, art censorship, prostitution, and pornography.

Independent Women's Forum (IWF)
1726 M Street, NW, Tenth Floor, Washington, DC   20036
(202) 419-1820
e-mail: info@iwf.org
Web site: www.iwf.org

IWF is a non-partisan, non-profit organization founded in 1992. IWF's mission is to rebuild civil society by advancing economic liberty, personal responsibility, and political freedom. IWF fosters greater respect for limited government, equality under the law, property rights, free markets, strong families, and a powerful and effective national defense and foreign policy. IWF's Web site includes position papers and news releases on a number of different topics, such as domestic violence, work and family balance, and women's healthcare.

National Organization for Women (NOW)
1100 H Street NW, 3rd Floor, Washington, DC   20005
(202) 628-8669 • fax: (202) 785-8576
e-mail: info@genocideintervention.net
Web site: www.genocideintervention.net

Since its founding in 1966, NOW's goal has been to take action to bring about equality for all women. NOW works to eliminate discrimination and harassment in the workplace, schools, the justice system, and all other sectors of society; secure abortion, birth control, and reproductive rights for all women; end all forms of violence against women; eradicate racism, sexism, and homophobia; and promote equality and justice in the United States. As the largest organization of U.S. feminist activists, NOW produces a great deal of scholarship and position statements, most of which can be found on its Web site. Recent titles include "Violence Against Women Statistics," "Who Needs an Equal Rights Amendment? You Do!" and "Equal Marriage NOW."

Older Women's League (OWL)
3300 North Fairfax Drive, Ste. 218, Arlington, VA 22201
1-800-825-3695 • fax: (703) 812-0687
e-mail: owlinfo@owl-national.org
Web site: www.owl-national.org

As the only national grassroots membership organization to focus solely on issues unique to women as they age, OWL strives to improve the status and quality of life of midlife and older women. OWL is a nonprofit, nonpartisan organization that accomplishes its work through research, education, and advocacy activities conducted through a chapter network. In addition to its annual Mother's Day Reports, OWL also regularly issues research that focuses on topics related to older women, for example, *The Color of Money: Retirement for Women of Diverse Communities* and *State of Older Women in America.*

Radical Women (RW)
New Valencia Hall, 1908 Mission St.
San Francisco, CA 94103
(415) 864-1278 • fax: (415) 864-0778
e-mail: NatRadicalWomen@aol.com
Web site: www.radicalwomen.org

RW views women's leadership as decisive to world revolution and trains women to take their place in the forefront of the struggle. RW is an autonomous, all-women's group, affiliated with the Freedom Socialist Party on the basis of mutual respect, solidarity, and shared socialist feminist ideals. RW produces many publications, including, *Three Asian American Writers Speak Out on Feminism, Woman as Leader: Double Jeopardy on Account of Sex,* and *The Radical Women Manifesto.*

Women Living Under Muslim Laws (WLUML)
PO Box 28445, London N19 5NZ
  UK
e-mail: wluml@wluml.org
Web site: www.wluml.org

Founded in 1987, WLUML is an international solidarity network that provides information, support, and a collective space for women whose lives are shaped, conditioned, or governed by laws and customs said to derive from Islam. WLUML collects, analyzes, and circulates information regarding women's diverse experiences and strategies in Muslim contexts using various media. In addition to a regular newsletter, the WLUML also publishes books and occasional papers, including *Great Ancestors: Women Asserting Rights in Muslim Contexts* and *Warning Signs of Fundamentalisms.*

Women's Freedom Network (WFN)
4410 Massachusetts Ave NW, Ste. 179
Washington, DC 20016
202) 885-6245
e-mail: wfn@american.edu
Web site: www.womensfreedom.org

WFN was founded in early 1993 by a group of women who were seeking alternatives to extremist ideological feminism and the anti-feminist traditionalism. It believes in the full participation of women in every area of American life. It celebrates the achievements women have already made, and it views women's issues in light of a philosophy that defines women and men as individuals and not in terms of gender. It does not set different standards of excellence, morality, or justice for men and women. In addition to position papers, WFN also publishes books, including *Women Working It Out: Career Plans and Business Decisions* and *Sexual Trafficking: An International Horror Story*.

Bibliography

The following articles have been selected to supplement the diverse views presented in this book.

Christian Akani — *Feminism and the African Woman.* Enugu, Nigeria: Fourth Dimension Publishing, 2006.

Elisabeth Badinter — *Dead End Feminism.* Malden, MA: Polity Press, 2006.

Leslie Bennetts — *The Feminine Mistake: Are We Giving Up Too Much?* New York: Voice/Hyperion, 2007.

Janet K. Boles and Diane Long Hoeveler — *The A to Z of Feminism.* Lanham, MD: Scarecrow Press, 2006.

Lynda Burns, ed. — *Feminist Alliances.* New York: Rodopi, 2006.

Estelle B. Freedman — *Feminism, Sexuality, and Politics: Essays.* Chapel Hill: University of North Carolina Press, 2006.

Geetanjali Gangoli — *Indian Feminisms: Law, Patriarchies and Violence in India.* Burlington, VT: Ashgate, 2007.

Wayne Grudem — *Evangelical Feminism: A New Path to Liberalism?* Wheaton, IL: Crossway Books, 2006.

Janet Halley · *Split Decisions: How and Why to Take a Break from Feminism*. Princeton, NJ: Princeton University Press, 2006.

Jane Hannam · *Feminism*. New York: Pearson/ Longman, 2007.

Joanne Hollows and Rachel Moseley, eds. · *Feminism in Popular Culture*. New York: Berg, 2006.

Nikki R. Keddie · *Women in the Middle East: Past and Present*. Princeton, NJ: Princeton University Press, 2007.

Amy Kesselman, Lily D. McNair, Nancy Schniedewind, eds. · *Women: Images and Realities: A Multicultural Anthology*. Boston: McGraw-Hill, 2008.

Laura Kipnis · *The Female Thing: Dirt, Sex, Envy, Vulnerability*. New York: Pantheon Books, 2006.

Gwyn Kirk and Margo Okazawa-Rey · *Women's Lives: Multicultural Perspectives*. 4th ed. Boston: McGraw-Hill, 2007.

Carrie L. Lukas · *The Politically Incorrect Guide to Women, Sex, and Feminism*. Washington, DC: Regency Publications, 2006.

Tara McKelvey, ed. · *One of the Guys: Women as Aggressors and Torturers*. Emeryville, CA: Seal Press, 2007.

Roxanne Newton   *Women Workers on Strike: Narratives of Southern Women Unionists.* New York: Routledge, 2007.

Kate O'Beirne   *Women Who Make the World Worse: And How their Radical Feminist Assault Is Ruining Our Families, Military, Schools, and Sports.* New York: Sentinel, 2006.

Catherine E. Rymph   *Republican Women: Feminism and Conservatism from Suffrage through the Rise of the New Right.* Chapel Hill: University of North Carolina Press, 2006.

Lisa H. Schwartzman   *Challenging Liberalism: Feminism as Political Critique.* University Park, PA: Pennsylvania State University Press, 2006.

Linda M. Scott   *Fresh Lipstick: Redressing Fashion and Feminism.* New York: Palgrave Macmillan, 2006.

Megan Seely   *Fight Like a Girl: How to be a Fearless Feminist.* New York: New York University Press, 2007.

Susan M. Shaw and Janet Lee, eds.   *Women's Voices, Feminist Visions: Classic and Contemporary Readings.* Boston: McGraw-Hill, 2007.

Evelyn M. Simien   *Black Feminist Voices in Politics.* Albany: State University of New York Press, 2006.

Erin Solaro	*Women in the Line of Fire: What You Should Know about Women in the Military.* Emeryville, CA: Seal Press, 2006.
Laura Sessions Stepp	*Unhooked: How Young Women Pursue Sex, Delay Love and Lose at Both.* New York: Riverhead Books, 2007.
Nelly P. Stromquist	*Feminist Organizations and Social Transformation in Latin America.* Boulder, CO: Paradigm Publishers, 2007.
Verta Taylor, Nancy Whittier, Leila J. Rupp	*Feminist Frontiers.* Boston: McGraw-Hill, 2007.
Teresa Zackodnik, ed.	*African American Feminisms, 1828–1923.* New York: Routledge, 2007.

Index